SIDE BY SIDE
Second Edition

SPANISH & ENGLISH GRAMMAR

Edith R. Farrell and C. Frederick Farrell Jr.

McGraw·Hill

New York   Chicago   San Francisco   Lisbon   London   Madrid   Mexico City
Milan   New Delhi   San Juan   Seoul   Singapore   Sydney   Toronto

The McGraw·Hill Companies

Library of Congress Cataloging-in-Publication Data

Farrell, Edith R., 1933–
    Side by side. Spanish & English grammar / Edith R. Farrell and C. Frederick Farrell,
Jr.—2nd ed.
        p.   cm.
    ISBN 0-07-141932-2
    1. Spanish language—Grammar, Comparative—English.   2. English language—
Grammar, Comparative—Spanish.   I. Title: Spanish & English grammar.   II. Title:
Spanish and English grammar.   III. Farrell, C. Frederick, 1934–   IV. Title.

PC4099.F37   2004
468.2′421—dc22   2004053870

To our parents and first teachers.

Acknowledgments
I remain thankful, as I know my late wife, Edith R. Farrell, would, to our colleague,
formerly at the University of Minnesota, Morris, Dr. Stacy Parker Aronson, for reading
the manuscript of this book; the Educational Development Program of the University
of Minnesota, which funded preliminary studies on which the companion volume of
this book was based; and David Stillman, who compiled the exercise section.

4 5 6 7 8 9 10 11 12   QPD/QPD   3 2 1 0 9 8 7 6 5 4

ISBN 0-07-141932-2

Table of Contents / Índice

PREFACE

*S*ide by Side Spanish & English Grammar presents the essential elements of Spanish grammar—the ones usually covered in a high school program or in the first year of college Spanish—"side by side" with their English counterparts. This comparative/contrastive approach allows students to build on what they already know, as they see the ways in which English and Spanish are similar, and to avoid potential trouble spots.

Side by Side Spanish & English Grammar is modeled on the French version, which has been used in both high school and university French classes, and even in some English classes for a few students who were having trouble in understanding their English grammar text. Its vocabulary is, for the most part, limited to the most frequently used Spanish words, so that students can concentrate on structure without being deterred by vocabulary problems.

It has been used as:

1. a reference book for beginning students, for whom the standard works are too complex to be useful. This allows them a means for independent inquiry.

2. a means of quick review of material forgotten over the summer or material missed because of illness.

3. a means of helping a student in a new school to catch up with the class.

4. a means of organizing or summarizing material presented in the primary text, especially for students whose learning style favors an "organized approach."

5. a means of providing a common background for talking about language with students who have studied English in different ways, so that their study of Spanish will show them something of how language works—one of the expectations of many college language requirements.

6. a source of an alternate way of explaining grammatical points in both English and Spanish to relieve the classroom teacher of the task.

Special features of the book that you and your students may find useful include:

1. a standard format in each section, which introduces the part of speech and answers the most common questions about it.

2. Quick-Check Charts (marked by a ✔) that allow students to write and express themselves with more confidence since they can independently check their sentences against a model.

3. appendices that identify and summarize trouble spots, such as the differences between interrogative pronouns and adjectives, and the uses of *ser* and *estar, por* and *para*.

4. an exercise section (with answer key), new to this edition, that tests understanding of the key grammatical concepts.

We hope that this text will provide ways for you and your students to increase independent work and to adapt material to different learning styles and situations.

INTRODUCTION

TO THE STUDENT

This manual grew out of a series of supplements to a grammar text. Its purpose is to help you learn Spanish more easily.

Many students have had trouble with foreign languages because they have not looked carefully enough, or critically enough, at their own. Struggles with your own language took place at such an early age that you have forgotten the times when it seemed difficult. Now it seems perfectly natural to you, and it is hard to adapt to different ways of expressing ideas.

Everything has been classified and arranged to show you your native language and your new language "side by side." You may be surprised at how many things are done the same way.

Information that is the same for both English and Spanish is usually *not* repeated on facing pages. If you find a section is omitted under the Spanish, look to your left and find it in English. If the English meaning of a Spanish example does not come right after that example, then it will usually be on the left-hand page too.

WHY GRAMMAR?

People can speak, read, or write their native language, at least to a reasonable degree, without studying formal grammar (the rules governing how we say, change, and arrange words to express our ideas).

Just by being around others, we hear millions of examples, and the patterns we hear become a part of us. Even babies start with correct basic patterns (subject-verb-object) even though words may be missing or incorrect: "Me wants cookie!"

Knowledge of grammar helps a great deal, though, in testing new and more complex words or patterns or in analyzing your writing to discover where a sentence went wrong or how it could be more effective. Sometimes being told, "It sounds right (or wrong)" won't help.

All of the explanations given in this book are of *standard* English or Spanish. Sometimes you may think, "I don't say that!" The important word here is "say." We often ignore some rules in conversation, or even in informal writing, such as friendly letters. At other times, though, if you are writing an important paper or giving a speech, you may want to use the standard form in order to make the best possible impression. You will also find that knowing grammar will help you in your study of language.

In learning a foreign language, grammar is necessary because it tells you how to choose the right word, or the right form of a word that you are using for the first time. It is not the way that you acquired your native language as a child, but it is an efficient way for adults who want to express more complex ideas and do not want to make any more mistakes than absolutely necessary.

Grammar saves you time and many mistakes by guiding you in your choices.

CHAPTER ONE

INTRODUCING

LANGUAGES

A Short
History
of
English

hat we now know as England was settled in the fifth and sixth centuries A.D. by Germanic tribes like the Angles, the Saxons and the Jutes, all speaking related, but distinct dialects. Later, in the ninth century, Scandinavian invaders came, bringing their languages, which also contributed to English. Political power determined the centers of learning, which contained the literature of continental Europe, written in Latin, as well as the contributions made by the inhabitants of Great Britain. By the ninth century, the primary center was in Wessex, due to the Viking invasions in the north, and so the West Saxon dialect became standard as Old English. It was heavily inflected, with endings on nouns to show many cases, and on verbs to show time and person.

This was the language current in 1066, when William the Conqueror, from the province of Normandy in what is now France, won the battle of Hastings and became ruler of England. The natives knew no French; William and his followers did not speak Old English. For a long time each group continued to speak its own language, but gradually they merged. Since the governing group spoke French, we often find that words for work, home, or plainer things come from Old English, while words for leisure or art products come from French.

Wamba, the jester in Sir Walter Scott's *Ivanhoe,* made a joke of this, saying that cows and pigs were Anglo-Saxon while the peasants took care of them, but became French (beef, pork) when they were ready to be eaten. In the same way, *house* looks and sounds like the German word *Haus,* but *mansion* looks like the French word for *house, maison.* We often have several words with a similar meaning. The more "elegant" one is frequently of French origin. For example, instead of *give* we may say *donate,* which is like the French *donner;* instead of *mean,* we may say *signify,* coming from *signifier.*

Latin, which remained the language of the church, and therefore of learning in general throughout all Europe, also had an influence on English. Around 1500, about 25% of the known Latin vocabulary was added to English. English, therefore, is basically a Germanic language, but one to which large portions of French and Latin were added.

Since Latin gave birth to both French and Spanish, and continued to exert an influence on both languages for many centuries, you will find that some English words with French or Latin roots have Spanish cognates. Compare the following:

Germanic root (Common)	French root (Elegant)	Latin root (Learned)
ask	question	interrogate
goodness	virtue	probity
better	improve	ameliorate
rider	cavalier	equestrian

Today English is recognized as an international language, and it has an impact on other cultures. The proximity of Latin America to the United States and the growing number of Hispanics in this country, however, have also given an increasingly important place to the Spanish language here. A number of Spanish words have come into everyday use in the United States. For example, words such as *tango, taco, hacienda,* and *barrio* are commonly used by Americans. Keep in mind, though, that these words may take on a more limited or even different meaning than their original Spanish definition.

A Short History of Spanish

Spanish is one of the Romance languages, like French, Italian, and others, that have grown out of Latin. Although there are some differences in the vocabulary and pronunciation of Spanish as it is spoken in Spain, Latin America, and other parts of the world, what we call Spanish is essentially derived from Castillian, the dialect of the historic Spanish province of Castile. As a result, many Spanish-speakers refer to the Spanish language as *el castellano*.

When the Romans invaded the Iberian Peninsula in the second and first centuries B.C., they encountered different peoples with different languages. When these colonized peoples learned Latin from the Roman soldiers they pronounced the words a little differently because they continued to use sounds that were familiar in their own languages. They also retained other important elements of their original languages, especially vocabulary. Other peoples, like those in northern Italy and Gaul (now France), did the same thing.

This continued until the "Latin" of different countries had evolved into different, although related, languages. While you can guess at words and even grammatical forms and rules in a different Romance language, based on your knowledge of another, a speaker of Spanish cannot be fully understood by a speaker of French, or vice-versa. As in English, Classical Latin provided Spanish, beginning in the sixteenth century, with a vocabulary stock that allowed it to be employed as a "learned" or literary language.

Following the Romans, the Visigoths and other Germanic tribes entered the Peninsula. Another early influence came from the Arabic-speaking Moors, who invaded Spain in 711 and inhabited most of it until the Reconquest of Spain was complete in 1492, when the Christians reclaimed the land. In that same year Jews and Muslims were expelled from Spanish soil, and Columbus arrived in what would become the Americas. The Moors left behind a lasting influence on many aspects of Spanish culture, including its architecture, music and dance, and the influence of Arabic can be seen in such words as *algebra, alfombra,* and *ojalá*.

The Spanish sound system evolved in significant ways as well. Italianisms were introduced, as they were throughout much of Europe, during the Renaissance. The French monarchy influenced eighteenth-century Spain, and resulted in overly-refined speech mimicking French. The nineteenth century continued to register modifications in the sound system, as well as grammatical transformations in the language. As the Industrial Revolution took hold, Spanish vocabulary adapted to accommodate the changing world it created.

All languages change, and the trend is to inflect them less and less. Distinctions that seem too hard or unnecessary to maintain die out. Different languages drop different things. For example, in Latin, and other older languages, every noun had gender, number and case (which told you its function, that is, how it was used in the sentence). German still has all three as very important elements.

In English, we pay little attention to grammatical gender, but nouns still have number (singular and plural) and one extra case (the possessive), while pronouns also have an objective case. The other cases are expressed by word order and prepositions. Spanish has no cases for nouns referring to things, but one can distinguish the subject from the object in the case of nouns referring to persons not only by word order but also by the preposition *a*, which normally precedes the object noun. Spanish keeps grammatical gender as well as number for all nouns. You will notice other instances in which Spanish and English emphasize different things. Let's look at a noun in Germanic languages:

	Modern German		**Old English**		**Modern English**
subjective	der König	die Könige	se cyning	tha cyningas	the king(s)
genitive	des König	der Könige	thoes cyning	thara cyninga	the king's(s')
dative	dem König	den Königen	thaem cyninge	thaem cyningum	to the king(s)
objective	den König	die Könige	thone cyning	tha cyningas	the king(s)

The declension (all the cases of a noun) in German is further complicated by having feminine and neuter nouns whose definite articles and endings are different from this masculine example, and irregular nouns, which have different rules. Adjectives also have different endings for each gender and case. For a verb sample, let's compare Latin and Spanish with English:

Latin		Modern Spanish		Modern English	
habeo	habemus	he	hemos	I have	we have
habes	habetis	has	habéis	you have	you have
habet	habent	ha	han	he/she has	they have

You will notice that there are some differences. In both Latin and Spanish the endings are so distinctive that it is not necessary to mention the subject. We think the Latin "h" was pronounced, but the "h" of most Romance languages, such as Spanish and French, is not. "V" and "b" are very similar sounds, and they change places easily. In Spanish they are almost identical. Of the five languages shown here, modern English is the least inflected.

CHAPTER
TWO

PARTS OF SPEECH

INTRODUCING THE PARTS OF SPEECH

B oth English and Spanish words are classified by "parts of speech." You may have learned these in elementary school without really seeing any use for them. They are important because different rules apply to the different categories. In your own language, you do this naturally, unless the word is new to you. You know to say: "one horse, two horses," adding an "s" to make it plural. You do not try to apply a noun's rule to verbs and say: "I am, we ams." Instead, you say: "we are." Using the wrong set of rules sometimes happens to people in a foreign language though, because all of the forms are new, and so none of them "sounds wrong." To avoid this kind of mistake, pay attention to the part of speech when you learn a new vocabulary word.

Parts of speech help you to identify words so that even if a word is used in several ways (and this happens in both English and Spanish) you can find the Spanish equivalent. *That,* for instance, can be:

1. a conjunction:

   I know **that** Mary is coming. → *Yo sé* **que** *María viene.*

2. a demonstrative adjective:

   That person is impossible. → **Esa** *persona es imposible.*

3. a pronoun:

   I didn't know **that.** → *Yo no sabía* **eso.**

When you know the parts of speech, you will not let the fact that a word is used several ways in English cause you to choose the wrong one in Spanish.

Here is a list of the parts of speech. The terms are defined by a traditional description, by the form that identifies them, and by their function (as the more modern structural linguists think of them).

NOUNS

1. Names or words standing for persons, places, things, abstracts:

   John, man, Madrid, city, table, justice

2. Words that usually become plural by adding "-s" or "-es" (along with a few other ways):

   book, books; fox, foxes; child, children

3. Words that serve as subjects, objects, or complements:

   Juan *is here. He reads* **the book.** *There is* **Carla.**

PRONOUNS

1. Words that substitute for nouns:

   John is already here. Do you see **him** *(John)?*

2. Words that are used when no noun is available:

   It *is raining.* **They** *say . . .* **You** *never know.*

3. Words that serve the same function as nouns:

   He *is here. He loves* **her.** *There* **it** *is.*

ADJECTIVES

1. Words that modify, limit, or qualify a noun or pronoun.

   large, red, unlucky, happy

2. Words that may be inflected (change form) or preceded by *more* or *most* to make comparisons:

   *large, lar**ger**, lar**gest**; serious, **more** serious, **most** serious*

VERBS

1. Words that express action or existence:

   speak, learn, run, be, have, seem

2. Words that can be inflected to show person *(I **am**, he **is**)*, time *(I **sing**, I **sang**)*, voice *(I **write**, it **is written**)*, and mood *(if I **am** here, if I **were** you)*.

ADVERBS

1. Words that modify verbs, adjectives, or other adverbs by telling how, when, where, or how much:

   *We'll come **soon**. It's **really** big. They do it **very** well.*

2. Words that can show comparison between verbs (as adjectives do for nouns):

   rapidly, more rapidly, most rapidly; quick, quicker, quickest

PREPOSITIONS

1. Words that express place, time, and other circumstances and show the relationship between two parts of a sentence:

   at, for, in, on, of, to

2. Words that are not inflected (words that never change form).

3. Words that have a noun or pronoun as their object:

   ***on** it, **in** a minute, **of** a sort*

These groups are called **prepositional phrases.**

CONJUNCTIONS

1. Coordinating conjunctions (*and, but, so,* etc.) connect words, phrases, or clauses that are grammatically equal:

   *John **and** Mary*

2. Subordinating conjunctions (*because, if, when,* etc.) connect subordinate clauses to the main clause:

   ***When** you see it, you will believe me.*

INTERJECTIONS

1. Exclamations:

   Hey! Wow! Alas.

2. Words that can be used alone or in sentences:

   ***Darn! Oh,** Wayne, is it true?*

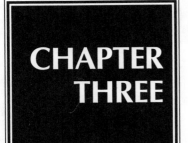

CHAPTER THREE

NOUNS

Introducing Nouns in English

WHAT ARE THEY? See the definitions on p. 10.

WHAT FORMS DO THEY HAVE?

NOTE: Nouns are often preceded by determiners (see p. 20):

> *a* book, *the* book, *my* book, *two* books

Nouns are considered to have **gender, number,** and **case.**

Gender. We use masculine or feminine gender only for something which is male or female:

> *man, woman, tigress*

All other nouns are neuter. Gender makes no difference in English except when there are two forms for one noun *(actor, actress)* or when the nouns are replaced by pronouns *(he, she, it).*

Number. Most nouns add "-s" or "-es" to the singular to form the plural. Some have irregular plurals:

> *mouse, mice; man, men; child, children*

Case. There is only one extra case in English, the possessive or genitive. It is formed by adding "-'s" to the singular or "s'" to plurals ending in "s:"

> ***Dawn's*** book, the ***book's*** pages, the ***chapters'*** titles

NOTE: We can also ignore the possessive case and use "of," although this form is less common when a person is involved.

> *the theories **of Kant,** the pages **of the book***

WHAT USES DO THEY HAVE? The three most common uses of nouns are as subjects, objects or complements. (see p. 18):

> ***Mrs. Gómez*** *is Spanish.* (subject)
> *He has a **pencil.*** (direct object of the verb)
> *She gave the hat to **Paul.*** (indirect object of the verb)
> *We are in the **room.*** (object of the preposition *in*)
> *It is a valuable **book.*** (complement)
> *Mrs. Gómez, a Spanish **woman,** is visiting us.* (appositive)
> *I have my **history** text.* (adjective)

(Continued on p. 16)

Introducing Nouns in Spanish

WHAT ARE THEY? See the definitions on p. 10.

WHAT FORMS DO THEY HAVE?

NOTES: Nouns are often preceded by determiners (see p. 20):
*un libro, **el** libro, **mi** libro, **dos** libros*
Nouns are considered to have **gender** and **number** but not **case.**

Gender. All nouns in Spanish are either masculine or feminine. There are no neuter nouns. You may think it is funny that in Spanish things are all either masculine or feminine. Speakers of Spanish and many other languages, such as French, German, and Russian can't understand why we don't think of neuter objects as masculine or feminine. When you learn a noun in Spanish, you must also learn whether it is masculine or feminine.

The gender of nouns is very important in Spanish, since their determiners and the adjectives accompanying them must be in the same gender. If a word is preceded by *el*, it is almost always masculine; *la* designates a feminine word. There is an exception for feminine words that begin with a stressed "a." To make pronunciation easier *el* is used. For example, we say el *agua*, even though *agua* is feminine.

Number. Spanish nouns that end in a vowel add "-s" to form the plural, but they also need a plural article. *Los* is the plural of *el* and *las* is the feminine plural. Nouns that end in a consonant add "-es" to make a plural.

Family names do not have a regular plural form. If they end in "s" or "z," the name remains unchanged, e.g., *los Rodríguez.* If they end in an unaccented vowel, you will find that sometimes the name is made plural *(los Castros),* but usually not.

Case. Nouns never change for case in Spanish. Possession is formed with the preposition *de* plus an article if one is needed:

*las teorías **de** Kant, las páginas **del** libro*

WHAT USES DO THEY HAVE? Nouns are used in the same way in Spanish as in English. Compare these sentences with the examples opposite.

La señora Gómez es española.
La señora Gómez, una **mujer** española, nos visita.
Él tiene un **lápiz.**
Ella le dio el sombrero a **Pablo.**
Estamos en el **cuarto.**
Es un **libro** valioso.
*Tengo mi texto **de historia.*** (Rarely is a noun used alone as an adjective in Spanish; a phrase, usually with *de*, is used.)

(Continued on p. 17)

Introducing Nouns
in English
(continued)

WHAT KINDS ARE THERE? There are a number of different classifications of nouns. Here are four important ones:

1. Common and **proper**

Common nouns are the words applied to a class of individuals. They begin with a lower-case letter:

student, country, cat, language

Proper nouns name a specific individual within a class. They begin with a capital letter:

Miss Jones, Mexico, Kitty, English

2. Countable and **mass**

Countable nouns are ones that can be counted:

one *pencil,* ***two*** *pencils*

Mass nouns describe a quantity that cannot be separated into individual components:

salt, weather

Introducing Nouns
in Spanish
(continued)

WHAT KINDS ARE THERE?

1. Common and **proper**

For the most part, nouns in Spanish are the same as in English, but there are a few important differences. Nouns for languages, days of the week, and months are common nouns. They do not require a capital letter.

English → *el inglés,*   Monday → *lunes,*   October → *octubre*

2. Countable and **mass**

These nouns follow the same principle in Spanish as in English. However, mass nouns such as *la gente* and *el pueblo* are always treated as singular.

INTRODUCING SUBJECTS AND OBJECTS

A. SUBJECTS

Subjects are most frequently nouns or pronouns. The subject of a verb is the person or thing that *exists* or *is doing* something:

> *Rochelle* and *I* are here. *Steven* speaks Spanish. Are *they* (the texts) arriving today?

✔ QUICK CHECK

☐ Ask yourself: *Who* is here? *Who* speaks Spanish? *What* is arriving?

The answer is the **subject.**

In normal word order, the subject comes before the verb. The subject is often, though not always, the first word in the sentence or clause.

B. SUBJECT COMPLEMENTS

These are words or phrases that define or complete our idea about the subject.

> *Mr. White is a* **professor.** *Jeanne and Alice are* **Americans.**

C. DIRECT OBJECTS

Some systems of grammar call these **object complements.** The name matters less than the ability to recognize their important function. Direct objects are usually nouns or pronouns that directly receive the verb's action. In normal word order the direct object comes after the verb:

> *Lana likes* **Jamal.**   *She likes* **him.**
> *The professor is giving a* **test.**   *He is giving* **it.**

✔ QUICK CHECK

☐ Ask yourself: Who *is liked?* What *is being given?*

The answer is the **direct object.**

D. INDIRECT OBJECTS

Indirect objects are usually nouns or pronouns that are indirectly affected by the verb's action. They indicate *to* whom or *for* whom something is done.

> *Speak* **to me***!*

Verbs of communication often have implied objects, e.g., tell me (the story). You may find these expressed in other languages.

COMBINATIONS

Some verbs (e.g., *give, tell, buy*) can have more than one object. Besides the direct object, there can also be an indirect object. With the subject, this can give you three nouns or pronouns with different functions even in a short sentence.

> *Robert gives* **the book** *to Alice.*
> (S.)   (D.O.)   (I.O.)

> *Robert gives* **Alice the book.**
> (S.)   (I.O.) (D.O.)

> *He gives* **it** *to her.*
> (S.)   (D.O.) (I.O.)

Notice that the two possible word orders do not have any effect on which object is direct and which is indirect. The word order in English does determine whether or not we use the word *to.*

✔ QUICK CHECK

☐ To analyze the sample sentences, ask:

Who gives? Answer: *Robert* or *he* → **subject**

Who or what is given? Answer: *the book* or *it* → **direct object**

To whom/for whom/to what/for what is it given? Answer: *Alice* or *her* → **indirect object**

E. OBJECTS OF PREPOSITIONS

We have learned that all prepositions must have objects (p. 11). These objects come immediately after the preposition:

*on the **table**, on **it**; after **Peter**, after **him***

NOTE: In questions and relative clauses (p. 76) this rule is often ignored in colloquial English, and we use the preposition alone at the end of the sentence:

***Who** did you give it **to**?* INSTEAD OF ***To whom** did you give it?*

The second sentence is standard English. Spanish uses the same patterns as in standard English.

PROBLEMS WITH DIRECT AND INDIRECT OBJECTS

English and Spanish verbs meaning the same thing usually take the same kind of object, but there are some exceptions. They must be learned as vocabulary items.

Direct Object in English

*It hurts **them**.*
*She taught **Charlie** to swim.*
*I asked **John** for a loan.*
*He fears **you**.*

Object of a Preposition in English

*They look at **the television**.*
*Helen is looking for **the book**.*
*Michael is waiting for **the train**.*
*Anne listens to **the radio**.*

Indirect Object in Spanish

***Les** duele.*
*José le enseñó a nadar **a Carlitos**.*
*Le pedí un préstamo **a Juan**.*
***Le** tiene miedo.*

Direct Object in Spanish

*Miran **la televisión**.*
*Elena busca **el libro**.*
*Miguel espera **el tren**.*
*Ana escucha **la radio**.*

Introducing Determiners in English

WHAT ARE THEY? Determiners are words that introduce nouns and their adjectives. They usually come first in a noun phrase:

the red book, *a* tall boy, *each* window, *several* students

WHAT KINDS ARE THERE? Many kinds of words can serve as determiners: definite articles, indefinite articles, numbers, general words like *each, either,* and *several,* along with several kinds of adjectives (possessives, demonstratives, and interrogatives), which will be discussed in the section on adjectives.

WHAT FORMS DO THEY HAVE? The **definite article** is always written *the,* but it is pronounced like *thee* before a vowel and some words beginning with "h" (e.g., *the book, the apple, the hour*). The **indefinite article** is *a/an* in the singular, *some* in the plural. *An* is used before words beginning with a vowel or silent "h." Other forms of determiners do not change either their spelling or their pronunciation.

WHAT USES DO THEY HAVE?

Definite Articles. *The* indicates a specific noun:

The book (the one you wanted) is on the table.

Indefinite Articles. *A/an* refer to any one of a class:

I see *a* boy. (not a specific one)

Others. Their use is determined by what you mean:

some boys, *few* boys, *several* boys, *ten* boys

Introducing Determiners in Spanish

WHAT FORMS DO THEY HAVE?

Definite Articles. The form of the definite article depends on the gender and number of the noun and, in the feminine singular, whether it begins with a stressed "a."

Gender/Number	Definite article	Before stressed "a"
Masculine singular	el	
Feminine singular	la	el
Masculine plural	los	
Feminine plural	las	

NOTE: These forms can also be combined with the prepositions *a* and *de* (see p. 77).

Indefinite Articles. These articles agree with the noun, just as the definite articles do. Just as *some* is the plural of *a/an* in English, so *unos/unas* express the notion of the English *some*. Compare the forms below:

Gender/Number	Indefinite article
Masculine singular	un
Feminine singular	una
Masculine plural	unos
Feminine plural	unas

Others. See also numbers, demonstrative and possessive adjectives, and indefinite words such as *cada* and *ninguno*. Each of the indefinite words must be learned separately as a vocabulary item. Some determiners change spelling for gender or number. Check this as you learn new words.

WHAT USES DO THEY HAVE?

Definite Articles are used:

1. before a specific noun, as in English, to express the word *the*.

2. before a noun used in a general sense:

   No me gusta la televisión. → I hate television (generally speaking).
   La guerra es mala. → War (in general) is bad.

3. before many nouns that take no article in English:

languages*	qualities	some countries**	titles	qualified proper names
el inglés	*la* belleza	*el* Perú	*el* general	*el* viejo México
				el Inglaterra del siglo XX
				la pequeña María

*After certain verbs such as *hablar* and *estudiar, el* is omitted.

**The most common countries whose names are preceded by a definite article are: *el Canadá, los Estados Unidos, el Perú, el Paraguay, el Uruguay, el Ecuador, los Países Bajos, el Brasil,* and *el Japón.* Even these do not always require the article in spoken Spanish.

(Continued on p. 22)

*Introducing
Determiners in
Spanish
(continued)*

Indefinite Articles are used to express the English words *a* or *an* in most situations and often their plural *some.*

> *un* grupo, *unos* grupos
> *una* ventana, *unas* ventanas

The indefinite article is sometimes omitted in Spanish when stating with the verb *ser* (to be) a person's profession, nationality, occupation, or religion. If a modifier is used, however, the indefinite article is generally used.

> *Es profesor.* → He is a teacher. BUT *Es **un buen** profesor.*
> *Es española.* → She is a Spanish woman. BUT *Es **una** española **muy guapa.***
> *¿Es usted estudiante?* → Are you a student? BUT *¿Es usted **un buen** estudiante?*

Others. Most other determiners are used as they are in English, except for those that change to agree with the noun in gender and number. Any differences will be noted in the vocabulary and/or a dictionary.

CHAPTER
FOUR

PRONOUNS

Introducing Pronouns in English

WHAT ARE THEY? See the definitions on p. 10.

WHAT FORMS DO THEY HAVE? Like nouns, pronouns have **gender, number,** and **case,** but more distinctions are made. They also change depending on the **person.**

Person. We distinguish between three persons. The **first person** is the one who is speaking *(I, me, we, us).* The **second person** is the one being spoken to *(you).* The **third person** is the one being spoken about *(he, she, it, they, them).* Both pronouns and verbs will be listed by person.

Gender. Some, but not all, pronouns can be distinguished by gender. *I* can refer to either a man or a woman. *She,* however, is always feminine, *he* always masculine, and *it,* even if it refers to an animal, is always neuter.

Number. Each of the three persons may be either singular or plural.

Case. Pronouns show more cases than nouns: the subjective, possessive, and objective *(I, mine, me; she, hers, her).* These will be discussed below.

WHAT USES DO THEY HAVE? Personal pronouns have the same functions as nouns. They may be:

1. subjects → **She** is here.
2. direct objects → I like **them.**
3. indirect objects → I am giving **him** the book.
4. objects of a preposition → The question is hard for **me.**
5. complements → It is **she** who is speaking.

WHAT KINDS ARE THERE? There are many different kinds of pronouns, each of which will be discussed individually:

1. **personal** (see p. 26)
2. **possessive** (see p. 30)
3. **reflexive** (see p. 32)
4. **disjunctive** (see p. 34)
5. **relative** (see p. 36)
6. **demonstrative** (see p. 40)
7. **interrogative** (see p. 42)

Introducing Pronouns in Spanish

Definitions and uses are the same in Spanish as in English. However, there are a number of other important things to know.

In Spanish, *you* has two commonly used forms in the singular: *tú* and *usted* and three in the plural: *vosotros, vosotras,* and *ustedes.*

1. **Tú** is the familiar form of *you,* related to the archaic English pronouns *thou* and *thee,* and is generally used for:

your peer group	small children
family members of your generation	animals
close friends	inferiors (it can be an insult)
fellow students (or colleagues)	God

   Usage varies in different Spanish-speaking countries and cultures, however. In some places, *tú* can be used when you first meet someone, and in others after getting to know the person better. There are some regions where *tú* is hardly used at all.*

2. **Usted** is universally recognized in the Spanish-speaking world as the polite or formal way to say *you. Usted* is abbreviated *Ud.* or *Vd.* Even though *usted* is used to address a second person, it is treated as a third-person form (like *él* and *ella*). Use this form for anyone who does not fall into one of the categories listed for *tú,* and especially for people older than you are. If you are uncertain about which to use, use *usted* first, then follow the lead of the native speaker.

3. **Vosotros** (m.) and **vosotras** (f.) are plural forms corresponding to *tú,* and can be used to address a group of people with whom you have a friendly relationship. They are used almost exclusively in Spain. You may come across these subject pronouns, or their object form, *os,* in your readings, but you are not expected to use them actively at this stage.

4. **Ustedes** is the plural form of *usted,* and is abbreviated *Uds.* or *Vds.* Besides being a formal way of addressing a group of people, *ustedes* replaces *vosotros/as* as the only second-person plural used in most Spanish-speaking countries and some parts of Spain, especially in the south. Like *usted, ustedes* requires its verb and corresponding pronouns to be in the third person.

* *Vos* is a second-person singular pronoun used in different regions of Latin America, especially Argentina, and is widespread throughout many other countries, such as Uruguay, Paraguay, Colombia, and Guatemala. It is a familiar way of addressing an individual, like *tú,* but it uses different verb forms. In modern Spain, Mexico, the Caribbean, and other parts of Latin America, *vos* is no longer a part of everyday speech.

Personal Pronouns in English

A. SUBJECT PRONOUNS (See p. 18.)

Person	Singular	Plural
1	I	we
2	you	you
3	he, she, it	they

John gives a present. → *He gives it.* (third person singular)
Mary and I arrive. → *We arrive.* (first person plural)

B. DIRECT OBJECT PRONOUNS (See p. 18.)

Person	Singular	Plural
1	me	us
2	you	you
3	him, her, it, one	them

He sees **me,** *and I see* **you.** *You found* **them.**

(Continued on p. 28)

Personal Pronouns in Spanish

A. SUBJECT PRONOUNS (Subjects of verbs; see p. 18.)

A subject pronoun must always be the same gender and number as the noun that it replaces.

Person	Singular	Plural
1	yo *(note lower-case "y")*	nosotros/nosotras
2	tú	vosotros/vosotras
3	usted	ustedes
	él (m.)	ellos (all male or mixed group)
	ella (f.)	ellas (all female group)

B. DIRECT OBJECT PRONOUNS (See p. 18.)

Person	Singular	Plural
1	me	nos
2	te	os
3	lo *(m.: you, him, it)**	los *(m.: them)*
	la *(f.: you, her, it)*	las *(f.: them)*

NOTE: Choosing the correct pronoun is easier if you remember that in the third person, three of the pronouns *(la, los,* and *las)* are the same as the definite articles.

> *Busco **los** libros.* → (Pronoun is **los**.) → **Los** *busco.*

Position. Except for affirmative commands and infinitives, the object pronoun in Spanish is placed directly before the conjugated verb of which it is the object.

*Él **me** ve.* → He sees me.   *Te veo.* → I see you.
Busco el libro. → I'm looking for the book.   *Lo busco.* → I'm looking for it.
Juana compra los libros. → Juana buys the books.   *Ella **los** compra.* → She buys them.
*No **lo** he visto.* → I have not seen it.

In a question or a negative sentence, the pronoun stays in this same position with respect to the verb, i.e., directly *before* it.

*¿Tienes los billetes? **Los** tienes?* → Do you have them?
*No tengo los billetes. No **los** tengo.* → I don't have them.

The only exceptions are affirmative commands, infinitives, and present participles. The pronoun follows these verb forms and is attached to them. In negative commands, the pronoun stays before the verb. (For additional comments on pronouns with commands see p. 113.)

Pedro quiere leer las cartas. → Peter wants to read the letters.
*Pedro **las** quiere leer.* OR *Pedro quiere leerlas.* → Peter wants to read them.
Dé el libro a María. → Give the book to Mary.
***Delo** a María.* → Give it to Mary. BUT *No **lo** dé a María.* → Don't give it to Mary.
Están preparándolos. → They are preparing them.
*No **los** están preparando.* → They are not preparing them.

* In Spain and in parts of Latin America, *le* is sometimes used in place of *lo* for the direct object pronoun *him.*

(Continued on p. 29)

Personal Pronouns
in English
(continued)

C. INDIRECT OBJECT PRONOUNS (See p. 18.)

Person	Singular	Plural
1	(to, for) me	(to, for) us
2	(to, for) you	(to, for) you
3	(to, for) him, her, it, one	(to, for) them

*He writes **her** a letter.*   *They send the letter **to us.***
*I bought a dress **for her.***   *I got **them** a ticket.*

D. OBJECTS OF PREPOSITIONS

After a preposition, we use the same form of the pronoun as for direct objects (before *me*).

NOTE: Beware of compound pronoun subjects or objects. They remain in the same case that would have been used for a single subject or object.

***I** am Spanish.*   ***She** and **I** are Spanish.*
*This is between **us.***   *This is between **you** and **me.***
*Give it to **me.***   *Give it to **him** and **me.***

E. WORD ORDER

When there are two pronoun objects in English, the direct object comes before the indirect:

*He shows **it** to **them.***

When using a noun and a pronoun together, word order can vary.

*He shows the **book** to **them.*** OR *He shows **them** the **book.***
        (D.O.)   (I.O.)   (I.O.)   (D.O.)

Personal Pronouns
in Spanish
(continued)

C. INDIRECT OBJECT PRONOUNS (See p. 18.)

The indirect object is used more frequently in Spanish where we would use a preposition plus an object in English.

Person	Singular	Plural
1	me	nos
2	te	os
3	le (m., f.)	les (m., f.)

These pronouns are in the same position in the sentence as the direct object pronouns.

*Él **le** escribe una carta.* → He is writing her/him a letter.
*No **me** envían una carta.* → They aren't sending me a letter.
*Mi mamá está **preparándome** la cena.* → My mother is preparing dinner for me.
*Ellos quieren **decirte** un secreto.* → They want to tell you a secret.
***Dime** la verdad.* → Tell me the truth. BUT *¡No **me** digas!* → Don't tell me! (You don't say!)

D. OBJECTS OF PREPOSITIONS

Most prepositions require the disjunctive pronouns in Spanish. (See p. 35.)

Person	Singular	Plural
1	mí	nosotros/nosotras
2	ti	vosotros/vosotras
3	usted	ustedes
	él, ella	ellos, ellas

1. *Pienso **en ella.*** → I am thinking of her.
2. *Pensamos a menudo **en ti.*** → We often think of you.

NOTE: With *con*, use the special forms *conmigo, contigo,* and *consigo.*

E. WORD ORDER OF PRONOUNS

Verbs often have more than one pronoun object.

***Nos lo** da.* → He gives **it to us.**

When there are two pronouns before the verb, use this order:

reflexive, indirect, direct

NOTES: When used before *lo, la, los,* and *las,* the indirect objects *le* and *les* become *se.* (that is, when both the direct and the indirect objects are in the third person)

*Pedro **le compra** los libros.* BUT ***Se los compra.***

Se has two uses, the one discussed in the note above, and as the reflexive pronoun (oneself). *Se* always stands first, whether it is a reflexive, direct, or an indirect object.

***Se lo** pone.* → He/she puts it on (him/herself). ***Se lo** dan.* → They give it to him/her.

(Continued on p. 30)

✔ QUICK CHECK OF NORMAL SPANISH WORD ORDER.

☐ When you write a sentence, check it with this chart to be sure you are right.

SUBJECT	+	me	+	lo
		nos		la
		te		los
		os		las
		se		
		le*		
		les*		

(VERB)

*These two forms, *le* and *les,* are used with the verb alone. They are replaced by *se* before *lo, la, los,* and *las.*

In affirmative commands, when the objects follow the verb, they are attached directly.

¡Démelo! → Give it to me!   *¡Muéstreselos!* → Show them to him/her!

See also p. 113.

Possessive Pronouns in English

WHAT ARE THEY? Possessive pronouns replace a possessive adjective (or a noun in the possessive case) combined with a noun.

*It's **my book.*** → *It's **mine.***   *It's **Anne's car.*** → *It's **hers.***

WHAT FORMS DO THEY HAVE? Possessive pronouns have person and number. In the third person singular, they also have gender. They do not have case. That is, they have the same form no matter what function they fulfill in the sentence.

Person	Singular	Plural
1	mine	ours
2	yours	yours
3	his, hers, its	theirs

As long as you know the person, gender, and number of the one who is the **possessor** (e.g., Mary), there is only one choice for the pronoun: hers.

*You have your book, where is **Mary's** book?* OR *Where is **her** book?*

To avoid repeating *book,* replace it and the possessive noun or adjective in front of it: *Mary's* and *her* are in the third-person feminine singular. Therefore, *hers* is the proper pronoun.

The sentence now reads:

*You have your book; where is **hers**?*

Possessive Pronouns in Spanish

WHAT FORMS ARE THERE? In Spanish, possessive pronouns have person and number as in English, but they also have gender changes. Person is a vocabulary problem and corresponds to the person who owns. Gender and number are determined by what is owned.

El libro de María → Mary's book   *su libro* → her book   *el suyo* → hers
las camisas de Juan → Juan's shirts   *sus camisas* → his shirts   *las suyas* → his

María requires a third person singular pronoun. *El libro* requires that the pronoun be masculine singular:

su libro → her book   *el suyo* → hers

Juan requires a third person singular pronoun, too. *Las camisas* requires that it be feminine plural:

sus camisas → his shirts   *las suyas* → his

Person	Singular	Plural
1	el mío, la mía, los míos, las mías	el nuestro, la nuestra, los nuestros, las nuestras
2	el tuyo, la tuya, los tuyos, las tuyas	el vuestro, la vuestra, los vuestros, las vuestras
3	el suyo, la suya, los suyos, las suyas	el suyo, la suya, los suyos, las suyas

NOTE: The possessive pronouns have the same forms, minus the definite article, as do the long forms of the possessive adjectives (see p. 57).

Note how the Spanish-speaking cultures express such phrases as: *a friend of mine* → *una amiga mía,* and *a book of yours* → *un libro tuyo.*

The possessive pronouns in English may be expressed in Spanish by the definite article plus *de,* plus the object pronoun in order to distinguish the meaning of *suyo/a:*

It is your book.   It is yours.   It is *her* book.   It is *hers.*
Es su libro.   Es el suyo.   Es su libro.   Es el suyo.
Es el libro de usted.   *Es el de usted.*   *Es el libro de ella.*   *Es el de ella.*

Reflexive/Reciprocal Pronouns in English

WHAT ARE THEY? The reflexive pronouns are defined as pronoun objects or complements that refer to the same person(s) or thing(s) as another element in the sentence, most frequently the subject.

WHAT FORMS DO THEY HAVE?

Person	Singular	Plural	Reciprocal
1	myself	ourselves	each other *or* one another
2	yourself	yourselves	each other *or* one another
3	himself	themselves	each other *or* one another
	herself		
	itself		
	oneself		

WHAT USES DO THEY HAVE? Reflexive pronouns are used as objects of a verb or a preposition.

WHAT KINDS ARE THERE? Reflexive pronouns are usually used only when the subjects act directly on themselves or do something to or for themselves directly.

Paul cut **himself.**   *I* told **myself** *it didn't matter.*

Occasionally, they are used idiomatically:

They always enjoy **themselves.**

For a mutual or reciprocal action, we use *each other* or *one another*. This expression does not change form:

They congratulated **each other.**   *We* talked to **each other** *yesterday.*
You two saw **each other** *last night.*

NOTE: Reflexive/reciprocal pronouns function as both direct and indirect object pronouns.

They saw **each other.** */ They talked to* **each other.**
        (D.O.)   (I.O.)

In English we often omit reflexive and reciprocal objects and expect everyone to understand what we mean:

We talked yesterday. (To each other is understood.)

Or we shift to a construction that requires no object:

Paul got hurt. (Hurt himself is understood.)

Consider the sentence:

We washed this morning.

It is meaningless if you have not heard the rest of the conversation. It may mean:

We washed ourselves (got washed). OR
We washed our clothes (did the laundry).

Reflexive/Reciprocal Pronouns in Spanish

WHAT FORMS DO THEY HAVE? They are the same as the direct and indirect object pronouns, except for the third person, and come in the same position in the sentence.

Person	Singular	Plural
1	me	nos
2	te	os
3	se	se

WHAT USES DO THEY HAVE? These pronouns are used as objects (either direct or indirect) of a verb. (see p. 18.) They can be either reflexive (directed to oneself) or reciprocal (directed to each other/one another).

Se hablan. → They are talking **to themselves.** OR They are talking to **each other.**

If the meaning is not clear from the context, a prepositional phrase plus *mismo* or *propio* can be added to indicate the reflexive. *El uno al otro,* can also be a sign of reciprocal use.

NOTE: Reflexive/reciprocal pronouns function as both direct and indirect object pronouns.

Él se mira a sí mismo. → He is looking at himself.
    (D.O.)
*Se hablan **el uno al otro.*** → They are talking to each other.
    (I.O.)

Many more reflexive verbs are used in Spanish than in English because transitive verbs must have objects. Contrast:

Lavamos el auto. → We wash the car.
Nos lavamos. → We wash ourselves.

Some Spanish verbs are reflexive in form only. Use the reflexive pronoun in Spanish, but do not translate it.

Me acuesto. → I'm going to bed.
La mujer se acerca. → The woman is approaching.

Many Spanish verbs can be used either reflexively or non-reflexively. Their meaning can be different depending on this form, e.g., *dormir* (to sleep) and *dormirse* (to fall asleep).

***Duermo** en la cama.* → I am sleeping in the bed.
***Me duermo** en la clase.* → I fall asleep in class.

Disjunctive Pronouns in English

WHAT ARE THEY? Disjunctive pronouns are not attached to a verb (disjunctive means "not joined"). They are used alone or as an extra word to give special emphasis and added intensity.

WHAT FORMS AND USES DO THEY HAVE? The forms these pronouns take depend on usage.

1. Used alone, the disjunctive pronoun is put in the subjective case in formal English (if required); and in the objective case in informal use:

   Who's there? I (formal) or *me* (informal).

2. As an intensifier, the forms of the reflexive pronoun are usually used:

   *I'll do it **myself.***   *He told me so **himself.***

3. Sometimes we merely raise our voices for emphasis:

   ***You** do it!*

Disjunctive Pronouns in Spanish

WHAT FORMS DO THEY HAVE? Disjunctive pronouns are used without verbs. When alone, they have the same form as the subject pronouns, but as objects of a preposition, they have the following forms:

Person	Singular	Plural
1	mí*	nosotros/as
2	ti	vosotros/as
3	él, ella, usted	ellos, ellas, ustedes
	sí *(reflexive)*	sí *(reflexive)*

WHAT USES DO THEY HAVE?

1. Use alone: *¿Quién es? ¡Yo!* → Who is it? Me!

2. Use with *mismo* for emphasis: *Yo **mismo** voy a hacerlo.* → I'm going to do it **myself.**

3. Use the special forms listed above after prepositions: *Eso es **para mí.*** → This is for me.

    With *con, mí, ti,* and *sí* are replaced by *-migo, -tigo,* and *-sigo: Hable **conmigo.*** → Talk with me.
    But use the subject forms after conjunctions:

    Rosa es más inteligente que nosotros. → Rosa is more intelligent than we are.

*Mí has an accent to distinguish it from the possessive adjective *mi* (*mi profesor* → my teacher).

Relative Pronouns in English

WHAT ARE THEY? Relative pronouns are words that begin a relative clause. They replace a noun called the **antecedent** and usually come directly after that noun.

WHAT FORMS DO THEY HAVE?

	Subject	Object	Possessive	Indirect Object/ Object of Preposition
Person	who (that)	whom (that)	whose	to (by) whom
Thing	which (that)	which (that)	whose (of which)	to (by) which where (for place prepositions) when (for time words)

To find the correct pronoun, you must know:

1. whether the antecedent is a person or a thing.
2. the function of the pronoun in the clause.
3. for subjects and objects, whether the clause is restrictive or nonrestrictive.

A **restrictive** clause defines the noun. *That* is used and the clause is not set off by commas:

*The book **that you just read** is world-renowned.*

Without the clause, you would not know which book was meant. It is an essential definition.

A **nonrestrictive** clause describes the noun rather than defining it. It is not necessary to form a complete sentence. *Who, whom,* or *which* are used and the clause is set off by commas:

*Don Quijote, **which the class is going to read,** is very famous.*

You could eliminate the relative clause, and the sentence would still make good sense. It is a nonessential description.

WHAT USES DO THEY HAVE?

1. Relative pronouns introduce clauses that give additional information about the antecedent.
2. They allow you to join two short sentences to make your writing smoother and to avoid repetition:

   Enrique González came yesterday. Enrique González is an expert pianist.

   *Enrique González, **who is an expert pianist,** came yesterday.*
3. They can be subjects, possessives, direct objects, indirect objects, or objects of a preposition in the relative clause.
4. Relative pronouns are inflected only for case, not person or number. Their form depends on their function in the clause.

NOTE: The function of the antecedent in the main clause has no effect on the choice of pronoun.

Relative Pronouns in Spanish

WHAT FORMS DO THEY HAVE?

	Subject	Object	Object of Preposition	Other
Person	que	que el cual*	quien(es)	cuyo/a
Thing	que	que	que	

*These forms must agree in gender and number with the antecedent. Only one example (masculine singular) is given here, but combinations of gender and number are possible. These forms are used if you need to distinguish gender or number, for instance if there are two nouns to which the relative pronoun may refer. Remember to use contractions with *a* and *de,* such as *al cual.* (See p. 77.)

Spanish does not use different pronouns to distinguish between restrictive and nonrestrictive clauses.

> *El libro que usted acaba de leer es famoso.* → The book **that you have just read** is famous.

> *Don Quijote, que la clase va a leer, es una novela famosa.* → Don Quijote, **which the class is going to read,** is a famous novel.

PROBLEMS:

1. Relative pronouns are often omitted in English, which Spanish does not allow. In the following English example, *whom* is omitted.

   Es el hombre que vi ayer. → That's the man I saw yesterday.

2. All relative pronouns must have antecedents. If there isn't one, you must supply *lo.*

   No llegó, lo que (or *lo cual*) *me sorprendió.* → He didn't come, which surprised me.

   Which does not refer to any specific noun, but to the idea (or fact) that he did not come.

3. Relative pronouns can take any verb form. This is true in English, too, but many people do not practice this.

   Soy yo que soy ansioso. → It is I **who am** worried.
   Somos nosotros que venimos. → We are the ones **who are** coming.

How to Analyze Relative Pronouns in English

Mr. Smith** is an excellent **cook.
(subject)   (complement)

Mr. Smith** made these **pies.
(subject)   (direct object)

1. Find the repeated element. → *Mr. Smith.*
2. Find the function of the repeated element in the second sentence, which will become the relative clause. → *subject*
3. Choose the relative pronoun. → *who* (person, subject)
4. Copy the first sentence through the antecedent. → *Mr. Smith . . .*
5. Put in the correct relative pronoun, in this case, *who.* → *Mr. Smith, who . . .*
6. Copy the relative clause. → *Mr. Smith, who made these pies . . .*
7. Copy the rest of the first sentence. Leave out any parts represented by the relative pronoun. → *Mr. Smith, who made these pies, is an excellent cook.*

Other examples:

The ten books are on the table. I am reading them.
*The ten books **that** I am reading are on the table.*

That is used because:

1. It is the object of *am reading* in the clause (no commas).
2. It refers to a thing.
3. It is restrictive (defines which ten books).

Mr. Jones died today. I saw him yesterday.
*Mr. Jones, **whom** I saw yesterday, died today.*

Whom is used because:

1. It is the object of *I saw* (with commas).
2. It refers to a person.
3. It is nonrestrictive (You already know who Mr. Jones is. This merely gives an extra fact about him.)

The student is asleep. I am speaking to that student.
*The student to **whom** I am speaking is asleep.*

To whom is used because:

1. It is the indirect object (no commas).
2. It refers to a person.
3. It is restrictive (defines which student).

The old house is falling down. I lived in that house as a child.
*The old house **where** (in which) I lived as a child is falling down.*

Where is used because:

1. It replaces a place preposition plus noun object (no commas).
2. It refers to a thing. (*In which* is also correct.)

(Continued on p. 39)

The woman lives in New York. I took her coat.
*The woman **whose** coat I took lives in New York.*

Whose is used because:

1. It is possessive (no commas).
2. It refers to a person.
3. It is restrictive (defines which woman).

How to Analyze Relative Pronouns in Spanish

The important considerations are *function in the clause* and *word order.*

La señora Sánchez es una periodista excelente. *La señora Sánchez* escribió estos ensayos.
   (subject)   (complement)   (subject)   (direct object)

1. Find the repeated element. → *La señora Sánchez*

2. Identify the function of the repeated element in the second sentence, which will become the relative clause. → *subject*

3. Choose the relative pronoun. → *que*

4. Copy the first sentence through the noun phrase to be described. → *La señora Sánchez . . .*

5. Put in the relative pronoun (with preposition, if any) to replace the second *La señora Sánchez.* → *La señora Sánchez, que . . .*

6. Copy the rest of the second sentence (now a relative clause). → *La señora Sánchez, que escribió estos ensayos, . . .*

7. Copy any other parts of the first sentence. → *La señora Sánchez, que escribió estos ensayos, es una periodista excelente.*

Try this with other sentences. Follow the same steps until they seem natural.

Los diez libros están en la mesa. Los estoy leyendo.
Los diez libros que estoy leyendo están en la mesa.

El señor Pérez murió hoy. Lo vi ayer.
El señor Pérez, al que vi ayer, murió hoy.

El estudiante está durmiendo. Hablo con este estudiante.
El estudiante a quien hablo está durmiendo.

La vieja casa se derrumbó. Vivía yo en esta casa durante mi juventud.
La vieja casa en la cual vivía durante mi juventud se derrumbó.

La mujer vive en Nueva York. Llevé la chaqueta de esa mujer.
La mujer de quien llevé la chaqueta vive en Nueva York.

This may seem complicated, requiring a lot of thought. That is because people usually use many short sentences when speaking. Relative clauses are used mainly to vary your written style—when you have time to think, cross something out, and write it in a different way.

Demonstrative Pronouns in English

WHAT ARE THEY? Demonstrative pronouns are words that point out someone or something.

WHAT FORMS DO THEY HAVE? There are only four forms for the demonstratives.

Singular	Plural
this (one)	these
that (one)	those

WHAT USES DO THEY HAVE? Demonstrative pronouns distinguish only between what is near *(this, these)* and far *(that, those)* and between singular and plural. No changes are made for gender or case.

I can't decide which of the chairs to buy.
This one *is lovely, but* ***that one*** *is comfortable.*
This *is lovely, but* ***that*** *is comfortable.*

Demonstrative Pronouns in Spanish

WHAT FORMS DO THEY HAVE?

	Gender	Singular	Plural
Group I	Masculine	éste, ése	éstos, ésos
	Feminine	ésta, ésa	éstas, ésas
	Neuter	esto, eso	
Group II	Masculine	aquél	aquéllos
	Feminine	aquélla	aquéllas
	Neuter	aquello	

NOTE: Other than *esto, eso,* and *aquello,* all of these forms are accompanied by an accent mark on the stressed vowel to distinguish them from demonstrative adjectives (*este, aquel,* etc.).

WHAT USES DO THEY HAVE? Demonstrative pronouns replace a demonstrative adjective plus its noun.

> *este / aquel hombre* → *éste / aquél*
> *esa / aquella mujer* → *ésa / aquélla*
> *estos / aquellos niños* → *éstos / aquéllos*
> *estas / aquellas niñas* → *éstas / aquéllas*

1. The forms *éste* and *ésta* translate the English expressions *this one* and *the latter. Éstos* and *éstas* translate as the pronoun *these,* and the expression *the latter.*

2. *Esto, eso* and *aquello* are used to translate the English indefinite pronouns *this* and *that. Aquello* translates as the indefinites *this* and *that.*

3. Forms of both *ése* and *aquél* translate as *that,* but *aquél* implies greater distance *(that one over there). Aquél* and *aquélla (aquéllos/aquéllas)* also translate as the expression *the former.*

Remember that the masculine and feminine forms of the demonstrative pronoun (used without the noun) are distinguished from the equivalent demonstrative adjective (used with a noun) by an accent mark placed on the stressed vowel.

✔ QUICK CHECK

	Demonstrative Adjective + Noun	Demonstrative Pronoun
Singular	este libro, aquel libro	éste, aquél
	esta casa, aquella casa	ésta, aquélla
Plural	estos papeles, aquellos papeles	éstos, aquéllos
	estas cartas, aquellas cartas	éstas, aquéllas
Neuter, singular		esto, eso, aquello

Interrogative Pronouns in English

WHAT ARE THEY? Interrogative pronouns are those used to ask a question.

WHAT FORMS DO THEY HAVE? Interrogative pronouns have different forms for people and things. The word referring to people, *who,* is also inflected for case.

	People	**Things**
Subject	who?	which? what?
Object	whom?	which? what?

No change is made for number. *Who? whom?* or *what?* can refer to one or to more than one

WHAT USES DO THEY HAVE?

1. Person, subject   **Who** *is coming? John.* or *The Smiths.*
2. Thing, subject   **What** *is going on? A riot?*
3. Person, direct object   **Whom** *did you see? John.*
4. Thing, direct object   **What** *are you doing? My homework.*
5. Person, indirect object*   **To whom** *are you speaking? To Mary.*
6. Person, object of a preposition   **With whom** *are you going? With Felipe.*
7. Thing, object of a preposition   **About what** *are you thinking? About the music.*

Which? is an interrogative pronoun related to choice. It can simply be *which?*, used in the singular or plural, or *which one(s)?*

Here are two books. **Which (one)** *do you want?*
There are many good shops in town. **Which (ones)** *do you like best?*

*NOTE: *To* or *for* indicate the indirect object. To review the indirect object, see p. 18.

Interrogative Pronouns in Spanish

WHAT FORMS DO THEY HAVE? Interrogatives are confusing in both English and Spanish because the same words are used for many things.

	Singular	Plural	English equivalent
Person	¿quién?	¿quiénes?	who? whom?
Thing	¿qué?	¿qué?	what?

NOTE: For distinctions in usage between *¿qué?* and *¿cuál(es)?*, see Appendix I, p. 121.

WHAT USES DO THEY HAVE?

1. In formal English many speakers make a distinction between *who?* (subject of the verb) and *whom?* (object of the verb). Spanish does not do this. *¿Quién* and *¿Quiénes?* are both subjects and objects of the verb.

2. The interrogative pronoun *what?* in English is both subject and object (of the verb or of the preposition). It does have different forms for gender and number.

3. In Spanish, *¿qué?* is both a subject and object of the verb and object of the preposition. Forms of *¿cuál?* do not change for these grammatical functions either, but there are different forms to show gender and number.

   1. Person, subject   *¿Quién (quiénes) llega(n)? María; Juan y María.*
   2. Thing, subject   *¿Qué pasa? Nada.*
   3. Person, direct object   *¿A quién(es) vio usted? A Lola y a Tomás.*
   4. Thing, direct object   *¿Qué haces? Leo el periódico.*
   5. Person, indirect object   *¿A quién(es) hablabas? A María.*
   6. Person, object of a preposition   *¿Con quién va usted al cine? Con Jesús.*
   7. Thing, object of a preposition   *¿En qué piensa usted? En la música.*

NOTE: Like the direct object noun indicating a person, the direct object form of the interrogative pronoun is preceded by the preposition *a*. (See #3 above.)

   Choice interrogatives ask for a choice: *Which one(s)?* These forms agree in gender and number with the noun they replace.

WHAT FORMS DO THEY HAVE?

	Singular	Plural	English equivalent
Person	¿cuál?	¿cuáles?	which one? / which ones?
Thing	¿cuál?	¿cuáles?	which ones(s)?
Masculine	¿cuánto?	¿cuántos?	how much? / how many?
Feminine	¿cuánta?	¿cuántas?	how much? / how many?

(Continued on p. 44)

WHAT USES DO THEY HAVE? Interrogative pronouns are used to choose among more than one possibility:

*Tengo tres **periódicos**. ¿**Cuál** prefieres?*
*Hay muchas **tiendas** cerca de la plaza. ¿**Cuáles** prefieren Uds.?*

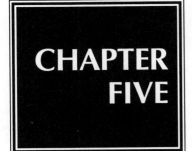

CHAPTER FIVE

ADJECTIVES

Introducing Adjectives in English

WHAT ARE THEY? See p. 11.

WHAT FORMS DO THEY HAVE? Some adjectives are invariable while other change form. These changes depend on the type of adjective. The types will be discussed separately below.

WHAT USES DO THEY HAVE? Primary uses of the adjective are:

1. as modifiers of nouns or pronouns.

2. as complements of either the subject or an object.

   Their function determines their position in the sentence:

1. As modifiers, the adjectives usually come before the nouns or pronouns:

   *Buy **that small white** house, or **the blue** one.*
        (adjectives) (noun)   (adjective) (pronoun)

2. As modifiers of indefinite pronouns, the adjectives follow:

   *Something **terrible** is happening.*
   (indef. pro.) (adjective)

3. As a subject complement, the adjective follows the verb *to be* or the linking verb, and describes the subject:

   *Mrs. Miller is **happy**. They seem **pleased**.*
      (to be)   (linking verb)

4. As an object complement, the adjective follows the direct object noun or pronoun:

   *That made the **exam hard**.   We considered **him crazy**.*
        (noun) (adj.)   (pronoun) (adj.)

WHAT KINDS ARE THERE? Each of the following types of adjectives will be discussed separately:

1. **Descriptive.**

2. **Proper** (a kind of descriptive adjective).

3. **Limiting** (includes **demonstratives, possessives, indefinites, interrogatives, numbers,** and **determiners.**

Introducing Adjectives in Spanish

WHAT FORMS DO THEY HAVE? Adjectives in Spanish agree in gender and number with the noun they modify. If an adjective describes a mixed group (masculine and feminine) then the masculine plural form is used.

WHAT USES DO THEY HAVE? Adjectives are used, as in English, as modifiers or complements, but their position in the sentence may be different. (See p. 49.)

Descriptive Adjectives in English

WHAT ARE THEY? Descriptive adjectives describe a noun or pronoun.

WHAT FORMS DO THEY HAVE? Many of them may be inflected to show comparison.

Descriptive Adjectives in Spanish

WHAT FORMS DO THEY HAVE?

1. Many descriptive adjectives in Spanish end in "-o" in the masculine singular and "-a" in the feminine singular. The plural of each of these forms is created by adding an "-s." The masculine singular form is the one listed first in vocabularies and dictionaries:

	Singular	Plural
Masculine	bueno	buenos
Feminine	buena	buenas

2. Most descriptive adjectives that do not end in "-o" or "-a" in the singular forms have the same form for both the masculine and feminine form. The plural is formed by adding "-es" to the singular unless the descriptive adjective already ends in "-e" in the singular. In this case add only "-s" to the singular form. For exceptions see "B" below.

   A. Examples of adjectives with only one singular form and their plurals

Singular	Plural	English Equivalent
fácil	fáciles	easy*
doble	dobles	double**
feroz	feroces	ferocious***

   B. Adjectives indicating a geographical division which end in a consonant form the feminine singular regularly; the masculine plural ends in "-es."

Masculine Singular	Feminine Singular	Masculine Plural	Feminine Plural
andaluz	andaluza	andaluces	andaluzas
español	española	españoles	españolas
portugués	portuguesa	portugueses	portuguesas
inglés	inglesa	ingleses	inglesas

* Other common adjectives that follow this pattern include: *difícil, útil, real.*
** Other common examples include: *pobre/pobres, grande/grandes, verde/verdes.*
*** Other common examples include: *audaz/audaces, capaz/capaces, sagaz/sagaces.*

Descriptive Adjectives in Spanish (continued)

NOTE:

1. Adjectives that end in *-án, -ón, -ín,* and *-or* form their feminine singular regularly. Comparative forms of the adjective (see page 51) ending in *-or* (*superior, ulterior,* etc.) have the same form in the masculine and feminine singular.

2. A small group of adjectives, not just descriptive ones, have a shortened form which is used before masculine singular nouns:

alguno → *algún*	**algún** *libro*
ninguno → *ningún*	**ningún** *libro*
bueno → *buen*	**buen** *tiempo*
malo → *mal*	**mal** *tiempo*
primero → *primer*	*el* **primer** *mes*
tercero → *tercer*	*el* **tercer** *mes*
uno → *un*	**un** *día*
santo → *San*	**San** *Juan* BUT **Santo** *Domingo;* **Santo** *Tomás* and *el* **santo** *padre*

3. The adjective *grande* becomes *gran* before most singular nouns of either gender; its meaning then becomes *great* rather than *big:*

   un **gran** *amigo; una* **gran** *amiga*

4. If two adjectives that have a short form are used before a singular noun, they both use the short form unless they are connected by a conjunction, like *and.*

WORD ORDER. Most descriptive adjectives in Spanish follow the noun. First you say what you're talking about: *una casa.* Then you describe it: *una casa* **blanca.**

1. A few adjectives change their meaning when they come before or after the noun:

Adjective	Before	After
antiguo/a	ancient	former
cierto/a	some	definite
diferente	unalike	various
nuevo/a	another	brand-new
pobre	pitiable	not rich
viejo/a	long-standing	aged

2. As you study Spanish you will find a number of adjectives whose English equivalent has the same meaning, but whose position in Spanish may vary with respect to the noun. In these cases the position before the noun suggests an inherent quality: *la blanca nieve* → white snow (snow is naturally white).

3. When there are two descriptive adjectives coming together, the one most closely associated with the noun comes first: *la pintura mexicana moderna* → modern Mexican painting.

4. Since some adjectives precede nouns and others follow, one must place them accordingly:

   a. *el* **famoso** *presidente* **norteamericano,** *Abraham Lincoln* → the **great American** president, Abraham Lincoln.

   b. *la* **gran** *escritora* **chilena contemporánea,** *Isabel Allende* → the **great contemporary Chilean** writer, Isabel Allende.

   c. *el cuento* **místico e interesante** → the **mystical and interesting** story.

   d. *la ciudad* **grande y hermosa** → the **great and beautiful** city.

Comparison of Adjectives in English

The three degrees of comparison are **positive, comparative,** and **superlative.**

1. Regular comparisons add *-er* and *-est* to short adjectives, sometimes with a change in spelling:

   short   *shorter*   *shortest*
   pretty   *prettier*   *prettiest*

2. Longer adjectives are compared by using *more* and *most,* or the negatives *less* and *least:*

   determined   **more** *determined*   **most** *determined*
   obvious   **less** *obvious*   **least** *obvious*

3. Some adjectives have irregular comparisons:

   good   *better*   *best*
   bad   *worse*   *worst*

4. Adjectives that cannot be compared include absolutes, which are by definition superlative. Uniqueness and perfection cannot be brought to a higher degree.

   unique, perfect

5. When a comparison is made, the following words introduce the second element:

   *He is taller **than** I (am).* (comparative)

   *He is the tallest boy **in** the class.* OR *He is the tallest **of all** of my students.* (superlative)

   If an adjective is already in the comparative, do not add *more* to it. Greater contrast may be expressed by words like *much* or *more:*

   Much smaller, **much more** difficult

Comparison of Adjectives in Spanish

1. Regular Spanish adjectives form the comparative with **más** (more), **tan** (as, showing equality), or **menos** (less) plus the adjective.

   más *grande,* **tan** *pequeño,* **menos** *importante*

2. Superlatives are formed with the correct definite article plus the comparative:

   *Es una casa **grande*** (positive)
   *Es una casa **más grande.*** (comparative)
   *Es **la** casa **más grande.** Es **la más grande.*** (superlative)

NOTE: The adjective remains in the same position, whether it is positive, comparative, or superlative:

   *un **gran** amigo; el **mejor** amigo; una cosa **más útil***

Comparison of Adjectives in Spanish (continued)

3. The most common irregular comparisons are:

bueno: **mejor** → better
malo: **peor** → worse
grande: **mayor** (or **más grande**) → greater, bigger
pequeño: **menor** (or **más pequeño**) → lesser, smaller

4. Adjectives that cannot be compared include absolutes, which are by definition superlative:

único/a, perfecto/a

Since uniqueness and perfection cannot be brought to a higher degree, we cannot use *el (la, los, las) más* with them.

5. When a comparison is made between two elements, use **que** with **más** or **menos,** and **como** with **tan** to link them.

(noun 1)	+ (verb)	+ (comp. word)	+ (adj.)	+ que/como	+ (noun/pronoun 2)
Jimena	*es*	*más*	*grande*	*que*	*María.*
Juan	*es*	*tan*	*grande*	*como*	*yo.*

For a superlative, use *de* to compare one to a group:

(noun/pronoun 1)	+ (verb)	+ (comp. word)	+ (adj.)	+ de	+ (noun/pronoun 2)
María/Ella	*es*	*la más*	*grande*	*de*	*su familia/ellos.*

✔ QUICK CHECK

Comparative construction: (1) *los hombres* (2) *las mujeres* (3) *ser grande/inteligente.*

(noun 1*)	+ (verb)	+ (comp. word)	+ (adj.)	+ (que)	+ (noun* 2)
Los hombres	*son*	*más*	*grandes*	*que*	*las mujeres.*
Los hombres	*son*	*tan*	*inteligentes*	*como*	*las mujeres.*

Superlative construction: (1) *Consuelo* (2) *la clase* (3) *ser lista.*

(noun** 1)	+ (verb)	+ (comp. word)	+ (adj.)	+ de	+ (noun* 2)
Consuelo	*es*	*la más*	*lista*	*de*	*la clase.*

Possibilities for error:

1. Word order (see Quick Check).

2. Verb (agreement with subject).

3. Adjective (agreement with the noun or pronoun it describes).

* The noun may be replaced by a noun phrase or a pronoun.
**or noun phrase or pronoun

Proper Adjectives in English

Proper adjectives are a kind of descriptive adjective formed from a proper noun (see p. 16):

Noun	Adjective
Rome	Roman
Shakespeare	Shakespearean

In English, both proper nouns and their adjectives are capitalized. Sometimes you cannot tell them apart by their form:

the **Spanish** (noun)   the **Spanish** people (adjective)

Limiting Adjectives in English

Limiting adjectives do not add to your knowledge of the noun, but they do direct you toward the right one by limiting the choices:

this chapter *(not another one)*
his book *(not hers)*
some people *(but not others)*
whose coat? *(the questioner wants to limit)*
the *second* lesson *(not the first)*

Under the heading of limiting adjectives these various subclasses need to be discussed separately.

Proper Adjectives in Spanish

Proper adjectives are formed from proper nouns in Spanish, but they are not capitalized:

romano/a → Roman   *venezolano/a* → Venezuelan

Limiting Adjectives in Spanish

See the discussion under the English forms.

Demonstrative Adjectives in English

WHAT ARE THEY? Demonstrative adjectives point out which of a group is (are) the one(s) that you are referring to.

WHAT FORMS DO THEY HAVE? They have the same forms as the demonstrative pronouns (see p. 40) and distinguish in the same way between near and far and between singular and plural:

	Singular	**Plural**
Near	this	these
Far	that	those

No agreement is needed for person, gender, or case. The demonstrative adjective precedes its noun:

This woman is talking to *that* man.
These little boys hate *those* dogs.

Demonstrative Adjectives in Spanish

WHAT FORMS DO THEY HAVE? Demonstrative adjectives agree with the noun they modify in gender and number.

Masculine Singular	Feminine Singular	Masculine Plural	Feminine Plural	English Equivalents
este	esta	estos	estas	this/these
ese	esa	esos	esas	that/those
aquel	aquella	aquellos	aquellas	that/those

WHAT USES DO THEY HAVE? The forms of *aquel* are used to express *that/those (over there)*. Otherwise use forms of *ese* for *that:*

aquella mujer → **that** woman (over there)
esa mujer → **that** woman (as opposed to **this** woman)
Esta mujer hablaba con *ese* hombre. → **This** woman was talking to **that** man.
Este hombre ama a *aquella* mujer. → **This** man loves **that** woman (over there).

Possessive Adjectives in English

WHAT ARE THEY? Possessive adjectives modify a noun by telling to whom or what it belongs.

WHAT FORMS DO THEY HAVE? Possessive adjectives tell the person, number, and gender (in the third person singular) of the possessor (the one who owns):

Person	Singular	Plural
1	my	our
2	your	your
3	his, her	their
	its, one's	

The adjectives do not tell us anything about the person or thing that is possessed.

Mr. Miller's son. → *his* son (third person, masculine, singular)
Mrs. Miller's son. → *her* son (third person, feminine, singular)
the Millers' son → *their* son (third person, plural)

WHAT USES DO THEY HAVE? The possessive adjective is always used with the noun:

my mother, *our* child, *your* turn

If you wish to omit the noun, you must use a pronoun, e.g. *mine, ours* (see p. 30).

Interrogative Adjectives in English

WHAT ARE THEY? Interrogative adjectives ask a question about limitation.

WHAT FORMS DO THEY HAVE?

1. Subjective and objective: *which? what?*

2. Possessive: *whose?*

   They are invariable, although they represent case.

WHAT USES DO THEY HAVE?

1. To ask a question:

   What assignment is for today? (subject)
   Which class do you have at 10? (object)
   Whose coat is this? (possessive)

2. As an exclamation:

   What a pretty house! **What** a job!

Possessive Adjectives in Spanish

Possessives are adjectives, so they agree in gender and number with the noun they modify, NOT with the person who is the owner.

WHAT FORMS DO THEY HAVE?

	Person	Singular	Plural	English Equivalent
Singular	1	mi	mis	my
	2	tu	tus	your
	3	su	sus	his, her, its, your
Plural	1	nuestro/a	nuestros/as	our
	2	vuestro/a	vuestros/as	your
	3	su	sus	your
				their

NOTES:

1. The adjectives *mi(s)*, *tu(s)* and *su(s)* have singular and plural forms, but no gender.

2. The adjectives *nuestro/a*, *nuestros/as* and *vuestro/a*, *vuestros/as* have both gender and number.

3. The adjectives *su/sus* have several English equivalents; therefore only a context can determine which English possessive adjective is meant.

   If the context is not clear, then use the noun plus *de* and a pronoun.

   el libro de María → *su libro* OR *el libro de ella*

4. *Your* is expressed by *su(s)* if the subject of the Spanish verb is *usted(es)*; by *tu(s)* if the subject is *tú*; by forms of *vuestro* if the subject of the verb is *vosotros/as*.

5. If you want to stress the possessive adjective, then place it after the noun and use the forms:

   mío(s), *mía(s)*, *tuyo(s)*, *tuya(s)*, *suyo(s)*, *suya(s)*, *nuestro/a*, *nuestros/as*, and *vuestros/as*.
   mi amigo → my friend AND *el amigo mío* → **my** friend

Interrogative Adjectives in Spanish

WHAT FORMS DO THEY HAVE? These adjectives are inflected for gender and number. They agree with the noun they modify.

Masculine Singular	Feminine Singular	Masculine Plural	Feminine Plural	English Equivalent
¿qué?	¿qué?	¿qué?	¿qué?	which? what?
¿cuál?	¿cuál?	¿cuáles?	¿cuáles?	which?
¿cuánto?	¿cuánta?	¿cuántos?	¿cuántas?	how much? how many?

NOTE:

1. As can be seen from the table above, the adjective *¿qué?* has only one form and therefore does not distinguish between singular and plural or between genders.

(Continued on p. 59)

Indefinite Adjectives in English

WHAT ARE THEY? Indefinite adjectives refer to nouns or pronouns that will not be defined more specifically:

Some students learn fast.   *Any* girl will tell you.
Both lectures are at 10.   *Each* (or *every*) class has its value.
I want *another* pen.   *Such* behavior is terrible.

WHAT FORMS DO THEY HAVE? These adjectives are invariable, i.e., they do not change their form. Some, however, may be used only with singular nouns *(each, every, another);* some only with plural ones *(both, other);* and some with either singular or plural *(some coffee, some people).*

Other Limiting Adjectives in English

A. ORDINAL NUMBERS

Ordinal numbers show the order in which things come.

One, two, and *three* (and all numbers ending in *1, 2,* and *3*) have irregular ordinals: *first, second, third*

All others form the ordinal by adding "-th:"

fourth, ninth, sixteenth

B. DETERMINERS. Determiners are often classified as adjectives. (See p. 20.)

Other Adjectival Forms in English

Many other kinds of words, even though they are not adjectives themselves, may be used as adjectives (i.e., to describe a noun or pronoun):

a *philosophy* professor (noun)
running water (present particle of a verb)
the *required* reading (past participle of a verb)
the poster *on the wall* (prepositional phrase)
the poster *that I bought* (relative clause)
I wondered what *to do.* (infinitive)
People *from all around* love him. (adverbial phrase)

Interrogative
Adjectives in
Spanish
(continued)

2. While the forms of the adjective *¿cuál?* distinguish singular and plural, the same forms are used for both genders.

3. The form of *¿cuánto?* reflects both the gender and the number of the thing(s) owned.

WHAT USES DO THEY HAVE?

1. To ask a question:

   *¿**Cuántos** libros tienes?*
   *¿**Qué** hora es?*
   *¿**Qué** trabajo tenemos para mañana?*
   *¿**Cuál** es el trabajo para mañana?*

2. As an exclamation:

   ¡Qué casa más bonita! ¡Qué lío!

Indefinite Adjectives in Spanish

***Algunos** estudiantes aprenden rápidamente.*
***Ambas** conferencias se reúnen a las diez.*
*Quisiera **otra** cosa.*
***Cualquier** mujer se lo dirá a usted.*

***Cada** ser humano es digno.*
***Todo** el mundo no cree eso.*
*¡**Tal** cosa es reprensible!*

Indefinite adjectives agree with their noun in gender and number, just as descriptive adjectives do.

Other Limiting Adjectives in Spanish

A. ORDINAL NUMBERS

Ordinal numbers are essentially vocabulary items in Spanish and need to be learned as such. They agree in gender and number with the noun they modify:

***primer** presidente; **primera** actriz; **quinto** tomo; **décima** lección*

B. DETERMINERS (see p. 21)

Other Adjectival Forms in Spanish

*la sala **de conferencias** (noun phrase)*
*la tía **querida** (past participle)*
*reloj **de pared** (prepositional phrase)*
*la ropa **que compré** (relative clause)*
*No sé qué **hacer.** (infinitive)*
*Los estudiantes **en todas partes** sienten admiración por ella. (adverb)*

CHAPTER SIX

ADVERBS

Introducing Adverbs in English

WHAT ARE THEY? See p. 11.

WHAT FORMS DO THEY HAVE? Adverbs formed from descriptive adjectives most frequently end in "-ly."

active, ***actively***   *slow,* ***slowly***

1. Like adjectives, adverbs may be inflected to show comparison:

Positive	Comparative	Superlative
actively	more actively	most actively
actively	less actively	least actively

The comparative is used to show the similarity or differences between how two people or things do something, or degrees of difference in qualifying an adjective or adverb. The superlative compares more than two. There must also be a word to tie the two points of comparison together.

*I walk **slowly**.* (positive)
*Jerry walks **more slowly than** I do.* (comparative)
*Monica walks **the most slowly of all**.* (superlative)

2. Some adverbs not ending in "-ly" may take "-er" and "-est," like adjectives:

*He runs fast, but I run **faster**.*   *Mary runs the **fastest** of all.*

3. Some adverbs from their comparison irregularly:

well	better	best
badly	worse	worst

WHAT USES DO THEY HAVE?

1. Adverbs answer the questions *how?, when?, where?,* or *how much?* about a verb, an adjective, or another adverb. Sometimes a phrase takes the place of a single adverb:

Yesterday *he came*	***here***	*and*	***very***	***quickly*** *told the story.*
(when)	(where)		(how much)	(how)
This morning *he went*	***there***			***by car.***

(Continued on p. 64)

Introducing Adverbs in Spanish

WHAT FORMS DO THEY HAVE? Most adverbs formed from descriptive adjectives add "-mente" to the feminine form of the adjective. Most of these are adverbs of manner.

activa (adjective)   ***activamente*** (adverb)

1. Like adjectives, adverbs may show comparison:

Positive	Comparative	Superlative
rápidamente	más rápidamente	lo más rápidamente
	tan rápidamente	
	menos rápidamente	lo menos rápidamente
naturalmente	más naturalmente	los más naturalmente

The words used to link the two elements being compared are the same as for adjectives. (See ✔ **Quick Check,** p. 51. The same pattern will work for adverbs.)

*Juan lee **rápidamente**.* (positive)
*Juan lee **más rápidamente** que Pedro.* (comparative of inequality)
*Mirta lee **tan rápidamente como Walter**.* (comparative of equality)
*Consuelo lee **lo más rápidamente** de todos los estudiantes.* (superlative)
*Rosita habla **lo más naturalmente**.* (superlative)

NOTE: The adverb, unlike the adjective, has only one form. Also note that in the superlative of the adverb (*lo* plus the comparative for unequal comparisons), it is the only form.

2. Some of the most common adverbs do not end in "-mente." They must be learned as vocabulary. They are compared in the same way as others:

Enrique se levanta temprano.   *Francisco se levanta **lo más temprano**.*
Juana llegó pronto.   *Juana llegó **tan pronto como yo**.*

3. Four adverbs form their comparison irregularly:

Positive	Comparative	Superlative
bien (well)	mejor	mejor
mal (badly)	peor	peor
mucho	más	más
poco	menos	menos

NOTE: The comparative and superlative forms are the same.

4. When making comparisons using verbs, use *tanto como* after the verb:

*Francisco no habla **tanto como** su padre.* → Francisco doesn't talk **as much as** his father does.

WHAT USES DO THEY HAVE?

1. See the uses in English, p. 62.

Ayer	*vino*	***aquí***	***y muy***	***pronto*** *nos relató lo que pasó.*
(when)		(where)	(how much)	(how)

(Continued on p. 65)

Introducing Adverbs
in English
(continued)

2. **Negatives.** Some adverbs make a sentence negative. These include words like *not, nowhere,* and *never.* In standard English, we may not use two negative words in one sentence unless we wish to express a positive, not a negative idea:

*He does**n't** have **no** friends, but he has **too few.***

The first clause used alone and intended as a negative would not be standard English. This includes not only negative adverbs, but nouns and adjectives as well.

3. **Questions.** Another group introduces questions: *when?, where?, how?,* and *why?* These are the questions that the majority of adverbs answer with respect to the verb, but the interrogative words themselves are adverbs, too:

When *does he arrive?*   **How** *do you know that?*

4. **Relative clauses.** The same adverbs that ask questions may also be used to form relative clauses. These clauses tell when, where, how, etc., the verb's action will take place and can be used in the same way:

*We are going to the movies **when** we finish our work.*

ADJECTIVES VS. ADVERBS

To be sure of choosing the correct word, it is essential to ask yourself:

Am I describing *someone (something)?* → **adjective**
Am I describing *how (when, where, why)* something is done? → **adverb**

*The **poem** is **good,** and the poet **reads** it **well.***
   (noun) (adjective)   (verb) (adverb)

*The **play** is **bad** and it's **badly performed.***
   (noun) (adjective)   (adverb) (verb)

This is especially important for verbs of mental or emotional state, or sensory verbs, which can be followed by either an adjective or an adverb. One of the most common examples is:

*I feel **bad.** (I am sick, unhappy.)*
*I feel **badly.** (My hands are not sensitive.)*

Introducing Adverbs
in Spanish
(continued)

2. Negatives

1. The negative word *no* in Spanish is an adverb and comes before

    a. a single verb: *No hablo inglés.*

    b. *haber, estar,* and *ser* when they are used in compound verb forms:

    No he visto a la maestra.

    No estamos trabajando mucho.

    c. object pronouns that precede verbs:

    No me gusta eso.

2. Other common negative adverbs that accompany verbs are:

    *no . . . jamás** → never
    *no . . . nunca** → never
    no . . . más → no longer
    *no . . . nada** → not at all
    *no . . . nadie** → no one
    no . . . ni . . . ni → neither . . . nor; or other ways to express two negatives in English

    No tengo **ni** tiempo **ni** dinero. → I have neither time nor money.

    No hablo **ni** a Juan **ni** a Pedro. → I speak neither to John nor to Peter.

    No leo **ni** hablo japonés. → I neither read nor speak Japanese.

    No tengo ese libro **ni** puedo comprarlo. → I don't have that book, nor can I buy it.

    * These words may come either before or after the verb. If they follow it, *no* must precede the verb:

    Nadie *me ama.* OR **No** *me ama* **nadie.** No one loves me.

    Nunca/jamás *hablo inglés en México.* OR **No** *hablo* **jamás** *inglés en México.*
    → I never speak English in Mexico.

    You can use several negatives in Spanish, which you can't do in standard English (although trying to is a common error):

    ¡No! ¡No digo **nunca nada a nadie!** → No! I never say anything to anyone!

3. Questions (Interrogative adverbs)

*¿**Cuándo** llegaste? Llegué ayer.*
*¿**Dónde** están los libros? Están en la mesa.*
*¿**Cómo** te llamas? Me llamo Aldo.*

4. Relative Clauses Used as Adverbs

Me acuesto **cuando termino mi trabajo.** (The clause answers the question, *when?*.)

ADJECTIVES VS. ADVERBS

El **poema** *es* **bueno** *y el poeta lo* **lee bien.**
  (noun)   (adj.)   (verb) (adverb)

El **libro** *es* **malo** *y todo el mundo lo* **comprende mal.**
  (noun) (adj.)   (verb) (adverb)

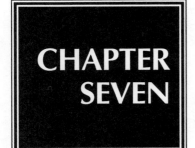

CHAPTER SEVEN

CONJUNCTIONS

Introducing Conjunctions in English

WHAT ARE THEY? See p. 11.

WHAT FORMS DO THEY HAVE? Conjunctions are function words; they are invariable.

WHAT KINDS ARE THERE? All conjunctions are linking words, but what is linked and the relationship between the linked parts determine to which of the three principle kinds of conjunctions a given one belongs: **coordinating, subordinating,** or **adverbial.**

WHAT USES DO THEY HAVE?

1. **Coordinating conjunctions** link two equal elements with the same grammatical construction. The two elements may be single words, phrases or entire clauses:

   John **and** Mary (nouns)
   *to be **or** not to be* (infinitives)
   *We came, **but** he was not there.* (independent clauses)

   NOTE: Words belonging to a subgroup of these conjunctions are called **correlatives.** The conjunctions occur in pairs:

   ***Both** John **and** Mary are in the class.*

2. **Subordinating conjunctions** do not join equal elements. One part is subordinated to the other. The conjunction introduces the subordinate clause (the one that cannot stand alone as a sentence):

   ***Although** he hurried, he was late.* (contrast)
   *We speak Spanish **when** the Rodríguez are here.* (time)
   ***Because** this course is easy, we all get A's.* (cause)

   Notice that the main idea of the sentence is in the main (independent) clause. The subordinate clause tells about the time, way, cause, or conditions involved and may show a contrast. Notice also that the main clause need not come first. You could reverse the order of the clauses in the examples above without changing the meaning of the sentence.

   There is also a subgroup of **correlative subordinating conjunctions.** Some of these are *if . . . then, so . . . that, etc.*:

   *That course is **so hard that** many fail.*

3. **Adverbial conjunctions** are sometimes called **conjunctive adverbs.** You can see from the names that grammarians are not sure whether they are really adverbs or conjunctions. Words or phrases like *therefore, perhaps, also, for example, as a result,* and *in other words,* fall into this category.

Introducing Conjunctions in Spanish

WHAT USES DO THEY HAVE?

1. Co-ordination:

*Juan **y** María* (nouns)
*Fernando **e** Isabel** (nouns)
*septiembre **u** octubre** (nouns)
*vivir **o** morir* (infinitives)
*Vinimos para verlo, **pero** no estuvo en casa.* (independent clauses)

*The conjunction *y* becomes *e* before another word beginning with an "e" sound (spelled "i-" or "hi-"); the preposition *o* becomes *u* before another "o" sound.

Correlatives are conjunctions made up of two or more elements. Here are some examples:

y . . . además	*Ella es bonita **y** fuerte **además.***
ni . . . ni	*No tenemos **ni** tiempo **ni** dinero.*
o . . . o	***O** nos vamos ahora **o** no vamos nunca.*

2. Subordination:

***Aunque** se dio prisa, no llegó a tiempo.* (contrast)
*Hablamos español **cuando** los Rodríguez están aquí.* (time)
*Somos ricos **porque** mis padres siempre han trabajado duro.* (cause)

Correlative subordinates:
*Este curso es **tan** difícil **que** muchos estudiantes se quejan de él.*

3. Adverbial conjunctions:

a menos que, dado que, desde que, hasta que, excepto que, mientras que, etc.

CHAPTER EIGHT

INTERJECTIONS

Introducing Interjections in English

WHAT ARE THEY? See p. 11.

WHAT FORMS DO THEY HAVE? Interjections are normally invariable vocabulary items.

WHAT USES DO THEY HAVE? Interjections are exclamations, often merely a sound (e.g., *ow!*) which are meant to convey emotion. They have no grammatical connection with the other words in the sentence. Set them off by commas.

Introducing Interjections in Spanish

Interjections present no serious problems in Spanish. They are simply vocabulary items that express exclamations. In Spanish, they are preceded by the inverted exclamation point ("¡") and followed, as in English, by an exclamation point. Some of the common ones are: *¡Ay!*, *¡Huj!*, *¡Hola!*, *¡Olé!*, *¡Caramba!*, *¡Cielos!*, *¡Dios!*, *¡Dios mío!*, *¡Anda!*, *¡Cuidado!*, *¡Alto!*, and *¡Caray!*

¡Qué! is also used in Spanish as an exclamation and translates as the English expression *what a . . . !* or just *what . . . !*:

¡Qué niña más bonita! → What a pretty girl!
¡Qué alegría! → What joy!

CHAPTER NINE

PREPOSITIONS

Introducing Prepositions in English

Prepositions, in any language, are very tricky words. Most of them have a basic meaning, but when they are used with other words, everything changes. You may think, for example, that you know what *up* means. Now consider this sentence:

*First he cut the tree **down**, then he cut it **up**.*

Foreigners learning English would be confused by that sentence. And it is not an isolated example. Take the case of a friend calling John's house early in the morning and asking for him. John's wife replies:

*He'll be **down** as soon as he's **up**.*

In other words, after learning a preposition, one must always be on the alert to see how it is used with other words. Often the meanings of one preposition will take several large pages of a good foreign language dictionary.

WHAT ARE THEY? See p. 11.

WHAT FORMS DO THEY HAVE? Prepositions are function words; they are invariable. They can be a single word or a group of words: *by, in spite of.*

WHAT USES DO THEY HAVE? Prepositions join a noun or pronoun (their object) to other words in the sentence and show its relation to them. In theory—also in formal English—a preposition is followed immediately by its object.

***to** the store; **about** the subject*

In practice—and in informal English, especially for phrasal verbs—we often leave the preposition until the end of the sentence:

*What is she waiting **for**?* INSTEAD OF ***For what** is she waiting?*
*This is the one that he is referring **to**.* INSTEAD OF *This is the one **to which** he is referring.*

Introducing Prepositions in Spanish

WHAT FORMS DO THEY HAVE? Most prepositions in Spanish are simply vocabulary items. They may be

1. one or several words: *en* → in, on; *al lado de* → beside, next to

2. they are invariable except for the two most common Spanish prepositions, *a* and *de*, which combine with the masculine singular definite article *el* to form *al* and *del*.*

    Voy al cine.
    Vengo del mercado. BUT: *Vengo a la casa de la profesora.*
    Es el libro del profesor.

NOTE: *Al* plus an infinitive translates to English as *upon* plus a gerund: *al hacer* → upon doing.

WHAT USES DO THEY HAVE?

1. Never expect a one-to-one equivalence between English and Spanish prepositions. They are capricious in both languages.

2. In English many verbs are followed by prepositions which change the meaning of the verb. In Spanish there are often, if not usually, two different verbs to express these two distinct notions:

    to look **for** → *buscar*   to look **at** → *mirar*   to look **into** → *investigar*

    Try to think of others and look them up in Spanish.

3. At times an English verb may be accompanied by a preposition when it has an object noun, but not when used alone. In Spanish such verbs are never followed by a preposition:

    In English: *Listen to the radio! Listen to it!* BUT *Listen!*
    In Spanish: *¡Escuche el radio! ¡Escúchelo!* AND *¡Escuche!*

4. In English you saw that the preposition comes before its object in formal speech and writing. In Spanish (and many other languages) it must always do so.

    Informal English: *Who are you going to the movies **with?***
    Formal English: ***With** whom are you going to the movies?*
    Spanish (formal or informal): *¿Con quién/es vas al cine?*

As noted above, you should never expect a one-to-one relationship. The same English word may be translated by more than one Spanish word. This is certainly true of prepositions as well as other words. If you ask: *How do you say "before" in Spanish?*, you need to know:

1. If it is a conjunction followed by a subject and verb (***before** someone did something).* In this case, it is *antes de que;*

2. If it is a preposition expressing location (***before** the door).* Then it is *delante de.*

3. If it is a preposition expressing time (***before** 3 o'clock).* Then it is *antes de.*

*This combining takes place even if the *de* is part of a longer expression: *en frente del edificio* → in front **of the** building.

(Continued on p. 78)

Introducing
Prepositions in
Spanish
(continued)

SOME SPECIAL PROBLEMS WITH PREPOSITIONS

1. For the uses of *para* and *por* meaning *for,* see Appendix II.

2. Other prepositions in Spanish.

   As we have seen, prepositions are essentially vocabulary items. It is important, though, to distinguish among some which are expressed by the same word in English:

   debajo de → under, underneath   *bajo de* → under (figuratively)
   sobre → on   *encima de* → on top of

3. Conjugated verbs are often followed by infinitives. If two verbs are used to express a single thought, the first will determine whether any preposition (and which one) will be used to introduce the infinitive. There can be more than two infinitives in a string (see the example below).

   Here is a list of some common verbs and the preposition they take when followed by an infinitive. Notice that in idiomatic expressions the English preposition may or may not be an equivalent of the Spanish preposition:

ir a	***Voy a*** *verlo mañana.* → **I'm going to** see him tomorrow.
venir a	***Vengo a*** *verlo mañana.* → **I'm coming to** see him tomorrow.
enseñar a	*El profesor me* ***enseñó a*** *traducir bien el francés.* → My teacher **taught me to** translate French well.
aprender a	*Yo* ***aprendí a*** *conducir el coche este verano.* → **I learned to** drive the car this summer.
enviar a	*Mi madre me* ***envió a*** *comprar unos vegetales.* → My mother **sent me to** buy some vegetables.
comenzar a	*La joven* ***comenzó a*** *reír.* → The young woman **began to** laugh.
ponerse a	***Me puse a*** *llorar.* → **I started to** cry.
llegar a	***Llegué a*** *aprender a hablar portugués.* → **I succeeded in** learning to speak Portuguese.

Verbs may also require a particular preposition before a noun or pronoun object. If you have not learned an expression, look it up. Here are some common ones:

dar a	*La ventana* ***da a*** *la plaza.* → The window **looks out on (faces toward)** the square.
felicitarse de	***Se felicitaron de*** *ganar el premio.* → They **congratulated themselves** on winning the prize.
reírse de	***Se rió de*** *mí.* → He **laughed at** me.
mirar por	***Miré por*** *la ventana.* I **looked out of** the window.
ocuparse en	*Nos* ***ocupamos en*** *nuestros estudios.* → We **are busy with** our studies.
acabar con	***Acabé con*** *la disputa.* → I **put an end to** the dispute.
acabar de	*Él* ***acaba de*** *verlos.* → He **has just** seen them.
acabar por	*Enrique* ***acabó por*** *darnos razón.* → Henry **finally** agreed with us.

Like verbs, some adjectives are followed by a preposition before a following infinitive. Spanish and English often use different prepositions:

último/a en	*Manuela es siempre la* ***última en*** *terminar.* → Manuela is always the **last one to** finish.
lento/a en	*Yo soy muy* ***lento en*** *aprender la química.* → I'm very **slow** at learning chemistry.
necesario/a para	*La física es* ***necesaria para*** *comprender el universo.* → Physics is **necessary for** learning about the universe.
listo/a para	*Yo estoy* ***lista para*** *la llegada de mis padres.* → I'm **ready for** my parents' arrival.

Other Examples:

*Voy **a** leer este libro.* → I am going to read this book.
*Comienzo **a** leer este libro.* → I am beginning to read this book.
*Trato **de** comenzar a leer este libro.* → I'm trying to begin to read this book.
*Voy **a** tratar **de** comenzar a leer este libro.* → I'm going to try to begin to read this book.
*Quiero tratar **de** comenzar **a** leer este libro.* → I want to try to begin to read this book.

CHAPTER TEN

VERBS

INTRODUCING VERBS

WHAT ARE THEY? See p. 11.

WHAT FORMS DO THEY HAVE? English has fewer inflected verb forms than other European languages. Many verbs have only four forms, e.g., *talk / talks / talked / talking;* some have five, e.g., *sing / sings / sang / sung / singing.*

In fact, in some systems of grammar, it is said that, technically, English has only two tenses—present and past—while other times are expressed by "periphrastic verbal constructions." This means that we use helping verbs and other expressions to convey differences. Here we will present verbs in a more traditional way, because it will help you to see the parallels between English and Spanish constructions. Here are the principal parts of a verb:

Infinitive	Simple Past	Past Participle	Present Participle
talk	talked	talked	talking
sing	sang	sung	singing

Some words that we use to identify verb forms are: **conjugation, tense, voice, transitive, intransitive,** and **mood.**

CONJUGATION has two meanings:

1. In Latin, and today in the Romance languages (like Spanish, Italian, Portuguese and French), verbs are classified into groups by their infinitive endings. English and German have only **regular** and **irregular,** sometimes called **weak** and **strong** verbs. Weak verbs take a regular ending to form the past: *talk/talked, follow/followed.* Strong verbs often change their vowel in the past or look completely different: *sing/sang, go/went.*

2. Conjugation also refers to a list, by person, of each possible form in a given tense. In Latin, there are six for every tense. The traditional example is *amare* (to love). Here is the present tense:

Person	Singular	Plural
1	amo I love	amamus we love
2	amas thou lovest	amatis you love
3	amat he loves	amant they love

Since each form is different, it is not even necessary to use a pronoun subject. The verb ending tells you who the subject is. The same is true for Spanish today.

In English we can conjugate verbs, but usually do not because there is only one inflected ending. We add an "-s" to the third person singular of the simple present tense:

Person	Singular	Plural
1	I speak	we speak
2	you speak	you speak
3	he/she speaks	they speak

We need to have the pronoun (or a noun) with every verb form, because otherwise we would not know who or what the subject is.

TENSE comes from the Latin *tempus,* via the French *temps,* meaning *time.* The tense tells you when something happened, how long it lasted, or whether it is completed.

VOICE can be **active** or **passive.** Active voice means that the subject is or is doing something.

> *Mary is happy. Mary reads the newspaper.* (*Mary* is the subject.)

Passive voice means that the subject is acted upon by an agent. The verb tells what happens to the subject:

> *The newspaper is read by Mary.* (*Newspaper* is the subject.)

TRANSITIVE VERBS are ones that require an object to express a complete meaning:

> *Mr. White surprised a burglar.*

Here, the verb *surprised* is transitive because it takes an object *(burglar).* If we left out the object, the sentence would not make much sense. It would be incomplete.

INTRANSITIVE VERBS are ones that do not require an object:

> *Paul sat down.*

Here, the verb *sat* is intransitive because it has no object; *down* is an adverb.

English has many verbs that can be either transitive or intransitive.

(subject)	(tr. verb)	(dir. obj.)
Peter	*eats*	*dinner at 7:00.*
The butcher	*weighs*	*the meat.*

(subject)	(intr. verb)	
Peter	*eats*	*at 7:00.*
The butcher	*weighs*	*a lot.*

MOOD tells about the mood, or attitude, of the speaker. Is the speaker stating a fact? offering a possibility that has not happened yet? making a recommendation? giving an order? For these we use different moods. They are:

indicative, imperative and **subjunctive**

The indicative is by far the most common. The other two moods are used in special circumstances which you will learn.

Introducing Questions in English

There are four ways to form a question in English:

1. Place a question mark after a statement and raise your voice when saying it aloud:

   Anne is here already?
   That's Mark's idea?

2. Add a "tag" repeating the verb or auxiliary verb as a negative question. In English the tag changes depending on the subject and the verb:

   *Peter is happy, **isn't he**?*
   *They came on time, **didn't they**?*

3. Invert the subject and an auxiliary or modal verb, or the verb *to be:*

   ***Do you** have any brothers?*
   ***Is Pablo** buying his books?* (present progressive)
   ***Does Pablo** buy his books?* (present)
   ***Has Pablo** bought his books?* (present perfect)
   ***May I** see you this evening?*
   ***Is Roberto** here today?*

4. Use an interrogative word:

   ***Where** is the library?*   ***When** does the library open?*

NOTE: At one time questions were often formed without an auxiliary, but that is less common now:

   Has Charles the book? has become *Does Charles have the book?*

Introducing Questions in Spanish

There are six ways to form questions in Spanish:

Simple tenses (in which the verb form consists of one word)

1. You may put in question marks before and after a statement and raise your voice at the end when saying it aloud. This is usually limited to conversations (oral and written):

    ¿Ana está aquí ya?

2. You may put *¿No es verdad?*, *¿verdad?*, or *¿no?* at the end of a statement with which you expect your listener or reader to agree:

    *Pedro está muy contento, **¿no es verdad?***   *Tienes dinero, **¿no?***

3. You may invert the noun or pronoun subjects of the verb when no object noun or adverb is present. You do NOT need an auxiliary to form a question, as you do in English:

    ¿Trabaja Juan?   *¿Estudian ustedes?*

4. You may invert by taking the noun subject and placing it after the verb's object noun, an adverb (if present), or an adjective that follows *ser* or *estar*.

    *¿Toca el piano **Miguel?***
    *¿Canta bien **Pablo?***
    *¿Era bonita **la niña?***

5. You may place the subject pronoun immediately after the verb when an object noun or pronoun is present:

    *¿Habla **usted** portugués?*

6. You may begin the sentence with an interrogative word:

    *¿**Dónde** está María?*
    *¿**A qué** hora se abre la biblioteca?*

Compound tenses

In compound tenses (those that use two or more words to form the verb), you may place the verb in front of the subject:

*¿**Ha visto** usted a Juan?*
*¿**Está cantando** Luisa en Nueva York o en Los Ángeles?*
*¿A qué hora **habría llegado** usted si no hubiera un tren?*

Note the difference in the position of the subject pronoun in the first sentence below and the subject noun in the second:

*¿Ha estado **usted** estudiando todos los días?*
*¿Han estado estudiando **los estudiantes** todos los días?*

Introducing Verbals in English

Verbals are forms of the verb that are not finite (i.e., do not agree with a subject and function as the predicate of a sentence). We will identify five kinds: **infinitive, past infinitive, gerund, present participle** (also called the **gerundive**), and **past participle.**

Present Infinitives in English

WHAT ARE THEY? The **present infinitive** is the basic form of the verb, the one you look up in a dictionary.

WHAT FORMS DO THEY HAVE? The infinitive is often identified by the word *to* preceding it. However, the *to* is omitted in many constructions, especially after verbs like *can* and *let*. Compare:

*I know how **to swim**. I can **swim**.*

Both sentences contain the infinitive of *swim*.

WHAT USES DO THEY HAVE? In addition to completing the verb, as in the above examples, infinitives may serve as subjects or objects of a sentence, as adjectives, or adverbs:

***To err** is human.* (subject)
*He hopes **to come** soon.* (object)
*English is the subject **to study**.* (adjective)
***To tell** the truth, he wants it more than ever.* (adverb)

Infinitives may also have their own direct objects and other modifiers:

*I am able **to do** that* (direct object) *easily* (adverb).

Past Infinitives in English

Past infinitives are formed with the present infinitive of the auxiliary (helping) verb and the past participle of the main verb.

to go (present infinitive) → *to have gone* (past infinitive)

They are used in the same way as the present infinitives (see above):

***To have quit** is terrible.*

Introducing Verbals in Spanish
Present Infinitives in Spanish

WHAT FORMS DO THEY HAVE? Spanish infinitives are grouped in three conjugations: those ending in "-ar," (the most common), "-er," and "-ir."

WHAT USES DO THEY HAVE?

*Ver es **creer**.* (subject or complement)
*Raúl **espera llegar** pronto.* (object)
*Voy a **decírselo** a tu padre.* (object of a preposition)
*El inglés es una lengua **para estudiar**.* (adjective)
***A decir** verdad, no lo creo yo.* (adverb)

Infinitives may have objects (either nouns, and their determiners, or pronouns) and be negated or otherwise modified:

*Voy a ver **el museo**.*
*Quiero comprender **mejor** la filosofía.*
*Voy a mostrárselo **a la señora García**.*
*Prefiero no llegar **a tiempo**.*

NOTES: Infinitives may have both a direct and an indirect object:

*Voy a **leerle** el periódico al señor Robles.*
*Voy a **leérselo**.*

Remember that *le* and *les* become *se* when used before *lo, la, los,* or *las.*

Past Infinitives in Spanish

WHAT FORMS DO THEY HAVE? Past infinitives are formed as in English with the present infinitive of the auxiliary *haber* plus the past participle:

Present	Past
estudiar	*haber estudiado*
vender	*haber vendido*
escribir	*haber escrito*

WHAT USES DO THEY HAVE? See uses for the present infinitive, but to express past time.

*Quería **haber escrito** una novela antes de morir.* → He wanted to have written a novel before dying.

Gerunds in English

WHAT ARE THEY? Gerunds are often called **verbal nouns.**

WHAT FORMS DO THEY HAVE? Gerunds end in *-ing.*

WHAT USES DO THEY HAVE? Gerunds have the same functions as other nouns. (See p. 14):

> *Walking is good for you.* (subject)
> *I like **singing.*** (object)

They may also have objects and modifiers:

> ***Making** money* (direct object) **quickly** (adverb) *is many people's goal.*

Participles in English

WHAT ARE THEY? Participles are verbal adjectives which constitute the third and fourth principal parts of a verb.

WHAT FORMS DO THEY HAVE?

1. Present participles end in "-ing:"

   *s**inging, talking, managing***

2. Past participles end in "-ed" or "-n" for regular verbs:

   tried, gathered, concentrated, given

   For irregular verbs, the past participle is the third principal part. To find it say: "Today I go; yesterday I went; I have gone; I am going." The form used after *I have* is the past participle. If you are not sure, look in the dictionary, the principal parts are given for every strong verb.

WHAT USES DO THEY HAVE? The two kinds of participles have basically the same uses:

1. As part of a compound verb (one requiring two or more words to form it):

   > *He **is talking.***   *They **have given.***

2. As adjectives:

   > *a **talking** doll*   *a **proven** fact*

3. In an absolute phrase:

   > ***Walking** along the street, he met Robin.*
   > ***Seen** from the front, the building was even more imposing.*

Gerunds in Spanish

The infinitive is used as the verbal noun in Spanish. See the first example above under the use of present infinitives. It may also be modified

Ganar dinero *rápidamente* es el objetivo de muchas personas.

Participles in Spanish

WHAT FORMS DO THEY HAVE?

1. Present participles are always invariable, that is, they do not change for gender or number.

    Most verbs whose infinitives end in "-ar" add "-ando," to the stem of the infinitive, after dropping "-ar:"

    hablar → *habl**ando***

    Verbs whose infinitive ends in "-er" or "-ir," add "-iendo:"

    aprender → *aprend**iendo***   *vivir* → *viv**iendo***

    "-ir" stem-changing verbs change "e" to "i" and "o" to "u" in the present participle:

    sentir → *s**i**ntiendo; pedir* → *p**i**diendo; dormir* → *d**u**rmiendo*

    The following verbs and their compounds (new verbs formed by adding a prefix to the basic verb) change the "i" of "-iendo" to "y:"

    caer → *ca**y**endo; destruir* → *destru**y**endo; traer* → *tra**y**endo;*
    creer → *cre**y**endo; ir* → ***y**endo; oír* → *o**y**endo,*

    and all other verbs ending in "-uir" or "-üir" (except those ending in "-guir.")

    Some common verbs have irregular present participles:

    venir → *v**i**niendo; decir* → *d**i**ciendo; poder* → *p**u**diendo*

    NOTE: Verbs ending in "-eír," like *reír* (laugh) and *sonreír* (smile) eliminate both the "e" and the accent mark:

    reír → ***riendo**; sonreír* → *sonr**iendo***

2. Most past participles in Spanish are formed by dropping the "-ar," "-er," or "-ir" from the infinitive and adding "-ado" to "-ar" verbs and "-ido" to "-er" and "-ir" verbs:

    hablar → *habl**ado**; vender* → *vend**ido**; pedir* → *ped**ido***

    There are a number of irregular past participles in Spanish. Here are some of the most common:*

decir	=	*dicho*	*poner*	=	*puesto*
hacer	=	*hecho*	*abrir*	=	*abierto*
morir	=	*muerto*	*cubrir*	=	*cubierto*
ver	=	*visto*	*escribir*	=	*escrito*
soltar	=	*suelto*	*romper*	=	*roto*
volver	=	*vuelto*			

* NOTE: Compounds of verbs normally form their past participles in the same way as the basic verb:

deponer/depuesto; revolver/revuelto; describir/descrito; entreabrir/entreabierto

(Continued on p. 89)

Indicative Mood

The verbs from pp. 88–109 are all in the **indicative mood.** It is the one used for stating facts or for making assertions as though they were facts.

Present Tenses in English

WHAT ARE THEY? The present tenses are defined by their uses, (see below).

WHAT FORMS DO THEY HAVE? Simple present, present progressive, and present emphatic.

1. **Simple present.** There is only one inflected form in the simple present. That is the third person singular, which adds "-s:"

Person	Singular	Plural
1	I sing	we sing
2	you sing	you sing
3	he/she sings	they sing

(Continued on p. 90)

Participles in Spanish (continued)

WHAT USES DO THEY HAVE?

Present participles are used:

1. with forms of *estar* to form the progressive tenses:

   *María **está cantando.***
   *Juan **estaba explicando.***

2. after the verbs *continuar* and *seguir* in place of an infinitive:

   *Julio **continúa aprendiendo** inglés.*
   *Ana **siguió leyendo.***

3. in a subordinate clause when its subject is the same as that of the main clause.

   ***Conociendo** muy bien la ciudad, Elena dio un paseo.*

   Be careful that you have the participle modifying the right noun. You know the problem of dangling participial phrases (in *I saw the church, walking up the hill,* who/what is walking?) Be sure you have the noun or pronoun to be modified next to the participial phrase.

4. Some nouns and adjectives with endings resembling that of the present participle were once verbals. Knowing that may help you to guess or remember their meanings:

   la vivienda → housing; *la hacienda* → ranch, fortune; *siguiente* → following; *ambulante* → walking

Past participles are used:

1. with forms of *haber* to form the perfect tenses:

   *Eduardo **ha terminado** su trabajo.*
   *Eduardo **había terminado** su trabajo.*

2. as adjectives:

   *el libro **abierto;** la Tierra **Prometida;** el Mar **Muerto***

3. as nouns:

   *el Valle de los **Caídos***

Indicative Mood

Look at the explanation of the indicative mood in English.

Present Tenses in Spanish

WHAT FORMS DO THEY HAVE? Unlike English, Spanish has only two forms of the present tense: the **simple present** and the **progressive.** The simple present form *hablo* may be translated as *I speak, I am speaking,* and *I do speak.* The progressive is used only if you wish to stress the fact the action is going on now: *estoy hablando* → I am speaking.

(Continued on p. 91)

2. Present progressive. This tense is formed with the present tense of *to be* plus the present participle:

Person	Singular	Plural
1	I am singing	we are singing
2	you are singing	you are singing
3	he/she is singing	they are singing

3. Present emphatic. This tense is formed with the present tense of the verb *to do* plus the infinitive:

Person	Singular	Plural
1	I do sing	we do sing
2	you do sing	you do sing
3	he/she does sing	they do sing

WHAT USES DO THEY HAVE?

The **simple present** is used for:

1. an action (or state) occurring in the present:

   *They **speak** Chinese.*

2. a habitual action (which is still true):

   *I always **study** in the evening.*

3. existing facts and eternal truths:

   *Madrid **is** the capital of Spain.*   *Time **is** money.*

The **present progressive** is used to:

1. stress the *continuing* nature of the verb's action in either a statement or a question:

   *I **am** still **trying!***   *Are you **going** to the library now?*

2. make a future action more immediate:

   *We **are reading** this book next week.*   *I **am going** to the show tomorrow.*

The **present emphatic** is used to:

1. add stress or contradict:

   *I **do want** to do well!*   *They **do** not **do** that!*

2. form questions or negative statements:

   *Do you **go** to the lake in the summer?*
   *I **do** not **know** what you are talking about.*

Present Tenses in Spanish (continued)

1. **Regular "-ar" verbs** (*hablar*). Drop the *-ar* and add *-a, -as, -a; -amos, -áis* or *-an:*

Person	Singular	Plural
1	hablo	hablamos
2	hablas	habláis
3	habla	hablan

For the present progressive tense, use the present tense of *estar* and the present participle, *hablando:*

Person	Singular	Plural
1	estoy hablando	estamos hablando
2	estás hablando	estáis hablando
3	está hablando	están hablando

NOTE: The verbs *ser, estar, ir,* and *venir* are never used in the progressive tenses.

2. **Regular "-er" verbs** (*aprender*). Drop the *-er* and add *-o, -es, -e, -emos, -éis,* or *-en:*

Person	Singular	Plural
1	aprendo	aprendemos
2	aprendes	aprendéis
3	aprende	aprenden

For the present progressive, follow the pattern for *-ar* verbs, but with the present participle ending in *-iendo: estoy permitiendo,* etc.

4. **Stem-changing verbs.** These changes occur as the result of a change in stress in the oral language.

"-ar" verbs

Stem vowel "e" becomes "ie;" "o" becomes "ue" in all forms except *nosotros* and *vosotros:*

pensar	*e → ie*	*pienso*	BUT: *pensamos*
mostrar	*o → ue*	*muestras*	BUT: *mostráis*
jugar	*u → ue*	*juega*	BUT: *jugamos*

"-er" verbs

Stem vowel "e" becomes "ie" and "o" becomes "ue" in all forms except *nosotros* and *vosotros:*

entender	*e → ie*	*entiendo*	BUT: *entendemos*
volver	*o → ue*	*vuelves*	BUT: *volvéis*
sentir	*e → ie*	*siento*	BUT: *sentimos*
dormir	*o → ue*	*duermes*	BUT: *dormís*

"-ir" verbs

Stem vowel "e" becomes "i" in all forms except *nosotros* and *vosotros:*

*repetir**	*e → i*	*repito*	BUT: *repetimos*

* Other common verbs following this pattern are *pedir, seguir, servir,* and *vestir.*

(Continued on p. 93)

Past Tenses in English

WHAT ARE THEY? The past tenses are used to describe actions (or states) in the past.

WHAT FORMS DO THEY HAVE? There are three past tenses corresponding to the three present tenses discussed previously. (For perfect tenses see pp. 100–109.)

The **simple past** is the second principal part of the verb (see p. 80). It is not inflected; all of the forms are the same. Weak verbs end in "ed" (e.g., *talked, walked*). Strong verbs are all irregular:

Person	Singular	Plural
1	I sang	we sang
2	you sang	you sang
3	he/she sang	they sang

The **past progressive** is formed by the simple past of the verb *to be* plus the present participle of the main verb.

Person	Singular	Plural
1	I was singing	we were singing
2	you were singing	you were singing
3	he/she was singing	they were singing

The **past emphatic** is formed with the simple past of *to do* plus the infinitive.

Person	Singular	Plural
1	I did sing	we did sing
2	you did sing	you did sing
3	he/she did sing	they did sing

WHAT USES DO THEY HAVE? The three past tenses in English closely parallel the three present tenses, except that the action takes place in the past. The simple past is a statement of a fact; the progressive emphasizes the duration or continuation of the action at a given moment in the past; the emphatic stresses the statement and is used to form negatives and questions.

OTHER PAST FORMS. There are also expressions that provide a special meaning:

IMMEDIATE PAST: *to have just* plus past participle:

Mary **has just arrived** this minute.

HABITUAL PAST action: *used to* or *would* plus infinitive:

I **used to go** to the movies every week.
For a long time **I would see them** every day.

REPEATED action: *kept (on)* plus present participle:

He **kept (on) doing** it.

Present Tenses in Spanish (continued)

5. Orthographic (spelling) changing verbs. Verbs in this group require a spelling change in the written language to reflect the need to keep the same sound throughout the oral forms of the present indicative.**

   a. *-ger* verbs *(escoger):* "g" becomes "j" in the first person singular: *escojo* BUT: *escoges, escoge,* etc.

   b. *-guir* verbs *(distinguir):* "gu" becomes "g" in the first person singular: *distingo* BUT: *distingues, distingue,* etc.

   c. consonant plus *-cer* verbs *(vencer):* "c" becomes "z" in the first person singular: *venzo* BUT: *vences,* etc.

   d. vowel plus *-cer* or *-cir (conocer):* "c" becomes "zc" in the first person singular: *conozco* BUT: *conoces,* etc. (Other examples include *ofrecer, parecer, producir,* and *traducir.*)

   e. *-fiar* and *-viar* and some consonant plus *-uar* verbs take an accent mark on the *i* or *u* on all written forms of the present indicative except the *nosotros* and *vosotros* forms, e.g.: *confío, confiamos, confiáis, confían; envía, enviáis, envían; continúo, continuamos, continúan; conceptúa, conceptuáis, conceptúan.*

6. Verbs that end in *-oy* in the first person singular:

   dar → doy; estar → estoy; ir → voy; ser → soy.

7. Common verbs that end in *-go* in the first person singular:

   decir → digo; hacer → hago; oír → oigo; poner → pongo; salir → salgo; tener → tengo; and *traer → traigo.*

** To make this easier, remember that in Spanish, as in English, the "c" is pronounced like "s" before "e" and "i:" *ciudad, centro.* Before other vowels, it has a "k" sound: *collar, cámara, curva.* This pattern will allow you to figure out which forms change, if you should happen to forget.

WHAT USES DO THEY HAVE?

1. All of the uses listed for the three present tenses in English may be filled by the simple present tense in Spanish. If you want to emphasize being in the act of doing something, use the present progressive.

2. Spanish also uses the present *hace* followed by a time expression plus *que* for an action begun in the past, but which is still going on in the present.

   Hace dos meses que *estudio español. →* I have been studying Spanish for two months (and I am still studying it).

Past Tenses in Spanish [Imperfect Tense]

WHAT FORMS DOES IT HAVE?

The imperfect tense of regular verbs is formed with a stem plus particular endings. The stem is formed by dropping the "-ar," "-er," or "-ir:"

Hablar	Perder	Salir
hablaba	perdía	salía
hablabas	perdías	salías
hablaba	perdía	salía
hablábamos	perdíamos	salíamos
hablabais	perdíais	salíais
hablaban	perdían	salían

(Continued on p. 94)

Past Tenses in
Spanish
(continued)

NOTE: There are only three verbs that are irregular in the imperfect: *ir, ser,* and *ver.* Note that it is only the stem that really presents a problem:

ir: iba; ibas; iba; íbamos; ibais; iban
ser: era; eras; era; éramos; erais; eran
ver: veía; veías; veía; veíamos; veíais; veían

The **imperfect progressive** is formed with the imperfect of *estar* plus the present participle:

Hablar	Perder	Salir
estaba hablando	estaba perdiendo	estaba saliendo
estabas hablando	estabas perdiendo	estabas saliendo
estaba hablando	estaba perdiendo	estaba saliendo
estábamos hablando	estábamos perdiendo	estábamos saliendo
estabais hablando	estabais perdiendo	estabais saliendo
estaban hablando	estaban perdiendo	estaban saliendo

WHAT USES DOES IT HAVE? Use the imperfect for:

1. description (What you are describing is more important than the action or is the background against which the action takes place. See the English *used to* construction.)
2. habitual action (describing something you used to do or kept on doing)
3. duration or continuing action (See the English past progressive.)

NOTE: You must choose the tense on the basis of these principles, not on a one-to-one correspondence with English tenses or idioms. The imperfect is used many times in Spanish when we would use the simple past in English:

Era lunes y llovía. → It was Monday, and it was raining. (description)

Yo asistía a Park Place School cuando era niña. → I went to Park Place School when I was a child. (habitual action/description)

Leía el periódico cuando sonó teléfono. → He was reading the newspaper when the telephone rang. (duration)

Isabel continuaba riéndose. → Isabel kept on laughing.

OTHER PAST TENSES. Other tenses used to describe past time are: **preterite** (p. 95); **present perfect** (p. 101); **present perfect progressive** (p. 103); **pluperfect** (p. 105); **past perfect progressive** (p. 105); **conditional perfect** (p. 109); **conditional perfect progressive** (p. 109) and **past subjunctive** (pp. 117–119).

Contrast the imperfect with the preterite, which is used for completed actions:

Preterite	Imperfect
Action happened (one or more times).	Action happened often (repeated/habitual)
Action is finished and completed.	Action is continuing, unfinished.
Action expresses a series of distinct events.	Action's purpose is primarily description.

María terminó sus deberes.	*María terminaba a menudo muy tarde.*
El teléfono sonó	*mientras que él dormía.*
Rodrigo llegó a Asunción, halló un hotel y se quedó allá	*Manolo era un estudiante mexicano que vivía en Texas pero que tomaba sus vacaciones en Santa Fe.*

OTHER PAST FORMS

1. For the immediate past, use the present tense of *acabar de* plus an infinitive:

   *María **acaba de llegar**.* → Mary has just arrived.

2. To express *had just* plus a past participle in English, use the imperfect tense of *acabar de* plus the infinitive:

   *Miguel **acababa de llegar**.* → Michael had just arrived.

3. For *used to* or *would* (in the sense of *used to*) plus an infinitive, use the imperfect tense of the verb:

   *Cuando yo **era** joven, yo **iba** al cine todos los sábados por la tarde.* → When I was young, I used to go (or would go) to the movies every Saturday afternoon.

Preterite Tense in Spanish

1. The **preterite tense** of the indicative mood is formed by dropping the infinitive endings and adding particular endings to the stem:

Hablar	Perder	Salir
hablé	perdí	salí
hablaste	perdiste	saliste
habló	perdió	salió
hablamos	perdimos	salimos
hablasteis	perdisteis	salisteis
hablaron	perdieron	salieron

2. There are several verbs with irregular preterite forms. Here are some of the most common:

andar	*anduve, anduviste, anduvo, anduvimos, anduvisteis, anduvieron*
caber	*cupe, cupiste, cupo, cupimos, cupisteis, cupieron*
dar	*di, diste, dio, dimos, disteis, dieron*
decir	*dije, dijiste, dijo, dijimos, dijisteis, dijeron*
dormir	*dormí, dormiste, durmió, dormimos, dormisteis, durmieron*
estar	*estuve, estuviste, estuvo, estuvimos, estuvisteis, estuvieron*
haber	*hube, hubiste, hubo, hubimos, hubisteis, hubieron*
hacer	*hice, hiciste, hizo, hicimos, hicisteis, hicieron*
ir	*fui, fuiste, fue, fuimos, fuisteis, fueron*
poder	*pude, pudiste, pudo, pudimos, pudisteis, pudieron*
poner	*puse, pusiste, puso, pusimos, pusisteis, pusieron*
querer	*quise, quisiste, quiso, quisimos, quisisteis, quisieron*
saber	*supe, supiste, supo, supimos, supisteis, supieron*
sentir	*sentí, sentiste, sintió, sentimos, sentisteis, sintieron*
ser	*fui, fuiste, fue, fuimos, fuisteis, fueron*
tener	*tuve, tuviste, tuvo, tuvimos, tuvisteis, tuvieron*
traducir	*traduje, tradujiste, tradujo, tradujimos, tradujisteis, tradujeron*
traer	*traje, trajiste, trajo, trajimos, trajisteis, trajeron*
venir	*vine, viniste, vino, vinimos, vinisteis, vinieron*

Verbs ending in "-car," "-gar," and "-zar" are irregular in the first person singular *(yo)* form only:

buscar → **bus**qué   *pagar* → **pa**gué   *empezar* → **empe**cé

(Continued on p. 97)

Future Tenses in English

WHAT ARE THEY? The future tenses are used to describe events that have not yet taken place.

WHAT FORMS DO THEY HAVE? There are only two tenses for future time: the **future** and the **future progressive.** Both are compound tenses, i.e., they require more than one word to form them. The future is formed by using the auxiliary verb *will* plus the infinitive of the main verb.

Person	Singular	Plural
1	I will sing	we will sing
2	you will sing	you will sing
3	he/she will sing	they will sing

The future progressive is formed with the future of *to be* plus the present participle. It therefore requires three words:

Person	Singular	Plural
1	I will be singing	we will be singing
2	you will be singing	you will be singing
3	he/she will be singing	they will be singing

NOTE:

1. There are no irregular future tenses in English.

2. *Will* and *shall* are often abbreviated as "'ll:"

   We'll do it tomorrow.   **You'll** be studying that next week.

3. In very formal English, a distinction is made between the first person forms and those of the second and third persons. *Shall* is used for the *I* and *we* forms:

   I **shall** sing, we **shall** sing.   We **shall** overcome.

4. It was this distinction between the two auxiliary verbs that used to allow us an emphatic future form. Reversing the normal auxiliaries *(I **will** speak!, They **shall** not pass!)* constituted the future emphatic. These forms, however, are now largely ignored.

WHAT USES DO THEY HAVE? The distinction between the future and the future progressive is the same as that between the corresponding tenses in the present (see p. 90). They are used:

1. to express an action or state that will happen or exist in the future.

2. in conditional sentences Type 1, when the *if* clause is in the present (See the ✔ **Quick Check,** p. 109.):

   If you **study,** you **will succeed.**

OTHER FUTURE FORMS. Another way of indicating future time is an idiomatic use of *to go.* The present tense of *to go* plus the infinitive of the main verb indicates future time:

   I **am going to sing** tomorrow.

Preterite Tense in
Spanish
(continued)

Verbs ending in "-ducir" follow the pattern of *traducir* above.

The **preterite perfect** is formed with the preterite of *haber* and the past participle. It is a literary form and is used only after time expressions:

> *Cuando Consuelo me **hubo hablado,** me di cuenta de que tenía razon.* → When Consuelo had spoken to me, I realized that she was right.

WHAT USES DOES IT HAVE? The preterite in Spanish is approximately equivalent to the simple past in English. It tells about completed action in the past. See p. 94 for its uses contrasted with those of the imperfect.

Future Tense in Spanish

WHAT FORMS DOES IT HAVE? There is only one future tense in Spanish. It is formed with the full infinitive plus particular endings.

NOTE:

1. The endings are the same for all verbs, even irregular ones. Any irregularities are in the stem. Once you know the stem, you know all of the forms.

2. All of the endings have an accent except for the *nosotros* form.

3. Future stems, regular and irregular, always end in "r."

Hablar	Perder	Dormir	Ser	Estar
hablaré	perderé	dormiré	seré	estaré
hablarás	perderás	dormirás	serás	estarás
hablará	perderá	dormirá	será	estará
hablaremos	perderemos	dormiremos	seremos	estaremos
hablaréis	perderéis	dormiréis	seréis	estaréis
hablarán	perderán	dormirán	serán	estarán

NOTE: There are a number of verbs with an irregular stem in the future. These stems are also used to form the conditional tense (see p. 99). Remember, all endings are regular in the future tense:

caber	**cabr**é		salir	**saldr**é
haber	**habr**ás		tener	**tendr**ás
poder	**podr**á		valer	**valdr**á
querer	**querr**emos		venir	**vendr**emos
saber	**sabr**éis		decir	**dir**éis
poner	**podr**án		hacer	**har**á

WHAT USES DOES IT HAVE? The future is used:

1. to express an action or state that will happen or exist:

> *Inés **llegará** en enero.* → Agnes will arrive in January.

2. in conditional sentences Type 1, when the "sí" clause is in the present. (See the ✔ **Quick Check,** p. 109.):

> *Si Uds. **estudian,** Uds. **saldrán** bien.* → If you study, you will succeed.

(Continued on p. 99)

Conditional Tense in English

WHAT IS IT? Many grammarians, even those who accept more than the present and the past as tenses, no longer consider the conditional to be a true tense, but rather a mood. This may be because its structure can convey a number of other meanings. We will consider it as a tense here, however, since it will help you to see the parallels with Spanish.

WHAT FORMS DOES IT HAVE? The **conditional** is formed with the auxiliary verb *would* plus the infinitive of the main verb:

Person	Singular	Plural
1	I would sing	we would sing
2	you would sing	you would sing
3	he/she would sing	they would sing

The **conditional progressive** tense is formed with the conditional of *to be* plus the present participle. It therefore requires three words:

Person	Singular	Plural
1	I would be singing	we would be singing
2	you would be singing	you would be singing
3	he/she would be singing	they would be singing

NOTE: The same distinction occurs with the conditional auxiliary as you saw with the future. In very formal English *should* is used in place of *would* for the first person forms (for example, **I should** *sing,* but **you would** not). However, confusion with *should* meaning *ought to* is a real problem here, and these forms have fallen into disuse. You will still find them occasionally, especially in older writing.

NOTE: *Would* and *should* are often abbreviated as "'d:"

I'd go if you did.

WHAT USES DOES IT HAVE? The conditional is used for:

1. conditional sentences Type 2 (See ✔ **Quick Check,** p. 109):

    *If I were rich,   (then)   I **would go** to Europe every year.*

    If ___(condition)___ , (then) ___(result)___ .

2. to convey the future from a past perspective.

    *On Sunday, John said, "OK, I **will see** you on Monday." (future)*
    *On Tuesday, Robert says, "John said that he **would see** us on Monday." (conditional)*

Future Tense in Spanish (continued)

3. as in English, as a command for the future:

   Presentarán *sus estudios el miércoles.* → You will give your reports on Wednesday.
   *No **matarás**.* → Thou shalt not kill.

4. to indicate possibility:

   *¿Quién **será**? **Será** tu hermano.* → I wonder who that is? It must be your brother.
   *¿**Será** posible?* → Is it possible?

OTHER FUTURE FORMS. As in English, we may use the present tense of *ir* plus *a* plus the infinitive of the main verb to express future time or intention in Spanish:

   Voy a cantar *mañana.* → I am going to sing tomorrow.

Conditional Tense in Spanish

WHAT IS IT? The **conditional** is often considered a mood, rather than a tense, in Spanish, since it expresses speculation, not facts. This distinction has, however, no practical effect on its forms or uses.

WHAT FORMS DOES IT HAVE? The conditional tense is formed with the same stem as the future for all regular verbs. The endings are the same as the imperfect for "-er" and "-ir" verbs (see p. 93).

Hablar (future: hablaré)	**Perder** (future: perderé)	**Dormir** (future: dormiré)
hablaría	perdería	dormiría
hablarías	perderías	dormirías
hablaría	perdería	dormiría
hablaríamos	perderíamos	dormiríamos
hablaríais	perderíais	dormiríais
hablarían	perderían	dormirían

NOTE: The same verbs that have an irregular stem in the future (see p. 97) also have an irregular stem in the conditional: *caber* → *cabría; saber* → *sabría; decir* → *diría.*

WHAT USES DOES IT HAVE? The conditional in Spanish is used in much the same way that it is in English:

1. to create conditional sentences Type 2 (See ✔ **Quick Check,** p. 109).

   Si yo fuera rico,   ***iría*** *a Europa todos los años.*
   Si ___(imperfect subjunctive)___ ,   ___(result) (conditional)___

2. to convey the future from a past perspective:

   *Pablo dice, "Bueno, **estudiaré** mañana."* → Pablo says, "OK, I will study tomorrow." (future)

   *Andrés dice, "Pablo dijo que **estudiaría** mañana."* → Andrew says, "Pablo said he would study tomorrow." (conditional)

3. to make a polite request:

   Querría *ir a Cuba.* → I would like to go to Cuba.

4. to express probability:

   Estarían *muy contentos.* → They were (probably) very happy.

Perfect Compound Tenses in English

WHAT ARE THEY? Perfect compound tenses express two ideas with one form:

1. the time of the action or state.

2. the fact that it is completed.

"Perfect" in this sense comes from the Latin *perfectus* meaning *finished* or *completed.* If something has been perfected, it does not need any further work. "Perfect" here, then, does not mean "ideal."

WHAT KINDS ARE THERE? There are four perfect tenses corresponding to each of the times we have already discussed: present, past, future, and conditional.

Present Perfect Tense in English

WHAT FORMS DOES IT HAVE? The present perfect is formed with the present tense of *to have* plus the past participle of the main verb:

Person	Singular	Plural
1	I have sung	we have sung
2	you have sung	you have sung
3	he/she has sung	they have sung

WHAT USES DOES IT HAVE? This tense indicates that from the point of view of present time, the action has been completed.

COMPARE:

*I **saw** that movie yesterday.*
*I **have seen** that movie.*

The first sentence is stressing a past action: *saw* or what I did yesterday. The second emphasizes that I am presently experienced with that movie, I now know what it is about, e.g., *I have* (present) *seen* (completed, finished with) *that movie.*

An idiomatic use of this tense is associated with the words *for* or *since:*

*I **have tried for** three hours to phone him.*
*I **have tried since** five o'clock to phone him.*

When we use the present perfect, we are implying that there is a momentary respite, but that the three hours of trying have lasted up to the present.

Perfect Compound Tenses in Spanish

WHAT FORMS DO THEY HAVE? All active voice perfect tenses, except the progressive tenses, are formed with a single auxiliary and the past participle of the main verb (see pp. 86–87 for forming the participles).

WHAT KINDS ARE THERE? In Spanish there is a perfect tense corresponding to each of the simple (one-word) tenses.

Present Perfect Tense in Spanish

WHAT FORMS ARE THERE? The present perfect is formed with the present tense of the auxiliary verb *haber* plus the past participle of the main verb:

Hablar	Perder	Salir
he hablado	he perdido	he salido
has hablado	has perdido	has salido
ha hablado	ha perdido	ha salido
hemos hablado	hemos perdido	hemos salido
habéis hablado	habéis perdido	habéis salido
han hablado	han perdido	han salido

WORD ORDER. For the most part, the auxiliary verb, the one that is conjugated, fills the same position as the simple-tense verb. Simply add the past participle ending to the verb stem:

✔ **QUICK CHECK**

Juan lo dice.   *Juan lo **ha dicho.***
Juan no lo dice.   *Juan no lo **ha dicho.***
¿Se lo dice?   *¿Se lo **ha dicho?***
¿No se lo digo a Juan?   *¿No se lo **he dicho** a Juan?*

WHAT USES DOES IT HAVE? The present perfect in Spanish is used much as we use it in English. It refers to an action which took place at an indefinite time or at a time period (long or short, a day or an historical period) which is still going on, and, especially, an action which still has an influence on the present.

***He aprendido** a nadar.* (I do not specify when I learned, and it is something that I can still do.)

*Este año **he aprendido** a nadar.* (This year is still going on.)

***He terminado** mis deberes.* (I am still finished with it.)

*Muchos **han leído** las obras de Cervantes.* (People have read, and are still reading, Cervantes' works.)

*Hasta ahora, no **he recibido** una carta del presidente.* (Up to now, I haven't, but I still may.)

(Continued on p. 103)

Present Perfect Progressive Tense in English

All progressive tenses emphasize duration, and all are conjugated with the auxiliary verb *to be* plus the present participle of the main verb.

WHAT FORMS DOES IT HAVE? To form the present perfect progressive, the verb *to be* is in the present perfect while the main verb is expressed by its present participle:

Person	Singular	Plural
1	I have been singing	we have been singing
2	you have been singing	you have been singing
3	he/she has been singing	they have been singing

WHAT USES DOES IT HAVE? As in other progressive tenses, this one emphasizes duration. Look at the example with *since* given previously (p. 100) for the present perfect. If, instead of *I have tried,* we had used *I have been trying for three hours to phone him,* we express not only a fact, but how long the three hours have seemed to us.

Present Perfect Tense in Spanish (continued)

Contrast the present perfect with the preterite:

*El año pasado, **aprendí** a nadar.* (Last year is over.)

***Terminé** mis tareas.* (The important thing is the past act of finishing, not what is happening now.)

*Hace dos años, los estudiantes **leyeron** las obras de Cervantes en esa clase.* (We are telling what they did.)

*No **recibí** nunca una carta del presidente.* (The occasion is past.)

In all of these examples the emphasis is on actions in the past. For other cases, you will need the imperfect. See p. 94 for a list contrasting the uses of these two tenses.

Present Perfect Progressive Tense in Spanish

WHAT FORMS DOES IT HAVE? To form the **present perfect progressive,** the verb *haber* is conjugated in the present, the verb *estar* is expressed by its past participle, and the main verb is in the present participle:

Person	Singular	Plural
1	he estado hablando	hemos estado hablando
2	has estado hablando	habéis estado hablando
3	ha estado hablando	han estado hablando

WHAT USES DOES IT HAVE? As in other progressive tenses, this one emphasizes duration:

***He estado esperándote** más de tres horas.*
***Uds. han estado quejándose** del trabajo toda la tarde.*
***Hemos estado pintando** la casa todo el día.*

Past Perfect (Pluperfect) Tense in English

WHAT IS IT? The **past perfect** tense tells us that some action (or state) was completed before some other past action (or state).

WHAT FORMS DOES IT HAVE? The past perfect tense is formed with the simple past of the auxiliary verb *to have* plus the past participle of the main verb:

Person	Singular	Plural
1	I had sung	we had sung
2	you had sung	you had sung
3	he/she had sung	they had sung

These forms are often contracted to *I'd, you'd,* etc.

I'd returned the book before you asked for it.

WHAT USES DOES IT HAVE? Think of past time sequence in terms of yesterday (past) and last week (further in the past):

Mary **had finished** her paper, before I **began** mine.
(past perfect; last week)   (past; yesterday)

Past Perfect Progressive Tense in English

WHAT IS IT? This tense shares the characteristics of the others that we have seen. It is:

past—viewpoint
perfect—completed
progressive—duration is stressed

WHAT FORMS DOES IT HAVE? The past perfect progressive tense is formed with the past perfect of the verb *to be* plus the present participle of the main verb:

Person	Singular	Plural
1	I had been singing	we had been singing
2	you had been singing	you had been singing
3	he/she had been singing	they had been singing

WHAT USES DOES IT HAVE? This tense expresses an action (or state) that had been continuing just before another past action:

*I **had been waiting** for three weeks when the letter **arrived.*** (The wait started three weeks and one day ago and continued up to yesterday, when the letter arrived.)

Past Perfect (Pluperfect) Tense in Spanish

WHAT FORMS DOES IT HAVE? The **past perfect** tense is formed with the imperfect tense of the auxiliary verb *haber* plus the past participle of the main verb:

Auxiliary	Past participle
había	hablado
habías	perdido
había	salido
habíamos	dicho
habíais	visto
habían	estado

WHAT USES DOES IT HAVE? Just as in English, the past perfect tense refers to something completed further back in the past than some other past action or state.

Preterite Perfect Tense in Spanish

WHAT FORMS DOES IT HAVE? The **preterite perfect** tense is formed with the preterite of the auxiliary verb *haber* plus the past participle of the verb:

Auxiliary	Past participle
hube	hablado
hubiste	perdido
hubo	salido
hubimos	dicho
hubisteis	visto
hubieron	estado

WHAT USES DOES IT HAVE? The preterite perfect tense is now used primarily in literature. The forms are given here in case you run across this tense in reading. The meanings are the same as for the past perfect, which you normally use for this time.

Past Perfect Progressive Tense in Spanish

WHAT FORMS DOES IT HAVE? The **past perfect progressive** tense is formed with the imperfect tense of *haber*, plus the past participle of *estar* and the present participle of the main verb.

(Continued on p. 107)

Future Perfect Tense in English

WHAT IS IT? This tense expresses action that will be completed at some time in the future.

WHAT FORMS DOES IT HAVE? It is formed with the future of the auxiliary verb *to have* plus the past participle of the main verb:

Person	Singular	Plural
1	I will have sung	we will have sung
2	you will have sung	you will have sung
3	he/she will have sung	they will have sung

NOTE: In spoken English, these forms are often contracted to *I'll've,* etc.

WHAT USES DOES IT HAVE? It is used to express future completion:

*I **will have finished** the book before the professor **gives** an exam.*
(future perfect)   (present)

NOTE: In the second clause, we use the present tense in English, but we are referring to the future. (The professor is not giving an exam now.)

Future Perfect Progressive Tense in English

WHAT IS IT? The **future perfect progressive** tense tells about an action (or state) that will be continued and then completed in the future.

WHAT FORMS DOES IT HAVE? It is formed with the future perfect tense of the auxiliary verb *to be* plus the present participle:

Person	Singular	Plural
1	I will have been singing	we will have been singing
2	you will have been singing	you will have been singing
3	he/she will have been singing	they will have been singing

WHAT USES DOES IT HAVE? It is used to emphasize the long duration of an action whose beginning is not specified but whose completion (at least provisionally) will be in the future:

*I **will have been studying** English for 16 years when I **graduate**.*
(future perfect progressive)   (present)

Although graduation is in the future, English uses the present tense. We do not know from this sentence when *I* will graduate, nor do we know in what year *I* started to study English. The important point is the relationship between the verbs in the two clauses. In other words, 16 years of study *will be completed* at the moment in the future when *I* graduate.

Past Perfect Progressive Tense in Spanish (continued)

Person	Singular	Plural
1	había estado hablando	habíamos estado hablando
2	habías estado hablando	habíais estado hablando
3	había estado hablando	habían estado hablando

WHAT USES DOES IT HAVE? As in English, this tense expresses an action that had been going on just before another past action.

*Habíamos estado esperando tres meses cuando por fin **llegó** la carta.*

Future Perfect Tense in Spanish

WHAT FORMS DOES IT HAVE? The **future perfect tense** is formed with the auxiliary verb *haber* in the future tense plus the past participle:

Hablar	Perder	Salir
habré hablado	habré perdido	habré salido
habrás hablado	habrás perdido	habrás salido
habrá hablado	habrá perdido	habrá salido
habremos hablado	habremos perdido	habremos salido
habréis hablado	habréis perdido	habréis salido
habrán hablado	habrán perdido	habrán salido

WHAT USES DOES IT HAVE? The future perfect tense is used:

1. as in English.

2. like the future to express surprise:

*¿Cómo lo **habrá sabido** Alonso?* → How can Alonso have known?

Future Perfect Progressive Tense in Spanish

WHAT FORMS DOES IT HAVE? It is formed with the future tense of *haber*, plus the past participle of *estar* and the present participle of the main verb:

Person	Singular	Plural
1	habré estado hablando	habremos estado hablando
2	habrás estado hablando	habréis estado hablando
3	habrá estado hablando	habrán estado hablando

WHAT USES DOES IT HAVE? It emphasizes the long duration of an action whose beginning is not specified but whose probable completion will be in the future, but is more often used to indicate possibility:

***Habrás estado estudiando** chino toda tu vida, ¿verdad?* → You've probably been studying Chinese all your life, right?

*¿**Habrá estado trabajando** Pedro en esa empresa por mucho tiempo?* → Is it possible that Pedro has been working in that company for a long time?

Conditional Perfect Tense in English

WHAT FORMS DOES IT HAVE? The **conditional perfect** tense is formed with the conditional tense of *to have* plus the past participle of the main verb:

Person	Singular	Plural
1	I would have sung	we would have sung
2	you would have sung	you would have sung
3	he/she would have sung	they would have sung

The forms of the auxiliary verb are often contracted in speech, to *I'd've, you'd've,* etc.

WHAT USES DOES IT HAVE? It is used primarily in the result clauses of Type 3 conditional sentences (see below):

He **would have (would've) seen** the film if **he had (he'd) known** that it was so good.
We **would have (would've) come**   if **we had (we'd) known** about it.
(conditional perfect)   (past perfect)

NOTE: The "'d" in English is a contraction of both *had* and *would*. This can cause some confusion unless you analyze what is meant:

If **he'd said** he needed it, **I'd've given** it to him.
(*he had said* [pluperfect]) (*I would have given* [cond. perf.])

✔ **QUICK CHECK.** The three most common types of conditional sentences:

If clause	Result clause	*If* clause	Result clause
1. If you **are** ready,	we **will** go.	present	future
2. If you **were** ready,	we **would** go.	subjunctive	conditional
3. If you **had been** ready,	we **would have** gone.	pluperfect	conditional perfect

Conditional Perfect Progressive Tense in English

WHAT FORMS DOES IT HAVE? The **conditional perfect progressive** tense is formed with the conditional perfect of the auxiliary *to be* plus the past participle of the main verb:

Person	Singular	Plural
1	I would have been singing	we would have been singing
2	you would have been singing	you would have been singing
3	he/she would have been singing	they would have been singing

WHAT USES DOES IT HAVE? This tense is used in the same way as the conditional perfect except that the idea of duration is added:

I **would not have been sleeping** when you arrived if **I had known** you were coming.
(cond. perf. prog.)   (past perf.)

Conditional Perfect Tense in Spanish

WHAT FORMS DOES IT HAVE? The **conditional perfect** tense is formed by the conditional of the auxiliary verb *haber* plus the past participle of the main verb:

Hablar	Perder	Salir
habría hablado	habría perdido	habría salido
habrías hablado	habrías perdido	habrías salido
habría hablado	habría perdido	habría salido
habríamos hablado	habríamos perdido	habríamos salido
habríais hablado	habríais perdido	habríais salido
habrían hablado	habrían perdido	habrían salido

WHAT USES DOES IT HAVE? The conditional perfect tense is used, as in English, primarily for Type 3 conditional sentences:

*Él **habría visto** la película, si él **hubiera sabido** que era tan buena.*

✔ **QUICK CHECK.** The three types of conditional sentences:

	Si clause	Result clause	*Si* clause	Result clause
1.	Si **está** listo	**iremos** al cine.	present	future
2.	Si **estuviera (estuviese)*** listo	**iríamos** al cine.	imperfect subjunctive	conditional
3.	Si **hubiera (hubiese)*** estado listo	**habríamos ido** al cine.	pluperfect subjunctive	conditional perfect

Conditional Perfect Progressive Tense in Spanish

WHAT FORMS DOES IT HAVE? The **conditional perfect progressive** tense is formed with the conditional of the verb *haber*, plus the past participle of *estar* and the present participle of the main verb:

Person	Singular	Plural
1	habría estado cantando	habríamos estado cantando
2	habrías estado cantando	habríais estado cantando
3	habría estado cantando	habrían estado cantando

WHAT USES DOES IT HAVE? This tense is used the same way as the conditional perfect, except that the idea of duration is added:

*No **habría estado durmiendo** cuando llegaste si **hubiera sabido** que venías.*
(cond. perf. prog.)   (pluperfect subjunctive)

* The *-se* forms of the imperfect subjunctive are used more in Spain than in Latin America.

Passive Voice in English

WHAT IS IT? The **passive voice** is the form used when the subject receives the verb action:

Active Voice:	**Subject**	**Active Verb**	**Direct Object**
	The **dog**	bit	**Susie.**
Passive Voice:	**Subject**	**Passive Verb**	**Agent**
	Susie	was bitten	by the **dog.**

Notice that the direct object of the active verb becomes the subject of the passive verb. The active verb's subject is placed after the passive verb in a prepositional phrase and is called the agent. It is not always expressed, as in the colloquial *John got caught.* It is either not important or not known by whom or what he was caught.

WHAT FORMS DOES IT HAVE? The passive voice is formed with *to be* or *get* plus the past participle of the main verb.

NOTE: Only transitive verbs (ones that have a direct object) can be made passive:

Time	Active	Passive
Present	Mary catches the ball.	The ball **is caught by** Mary.
Past	The man read the book.	The book **was read by** the man.
Future	Mrs. Smith will lead the discussion.	The discussion **will be led by** Mrs. Smith.
Cond. Perf.	The class would have finished, but . . .	The job **would have been finished by** the class, but . . .

All of the perfect and progressive tenses can be formed in the same way. Some of the forms can get very long (e.g., the passive future progressive reads: *The work **will have been being done** at 3:00 P.M.*) and are seldom used.

Passive Voice in Spanish

WHAT FORMS DOES IT HAVE? The passive voice in Spanish is always formed with the verb *ser* or sometimes *estar** plus the past participle of the main verb acting like an adjective (that is, always agreeing in gender and number with the subject.)
The passive voice may be in any tense and in either indicative or subjunctive mood.

* *Estar* is used when neither the agent nor the action is of any real importance. The past participle is, in effect, an adjective describing a condition, or the result of a past action:

*El apartamento **estaba** muy mal **amueblado.*** → The apartment was very badly furnished.

Passive Voice in Spanish (continued)

Agency (by) is usually expressed by *por.* Sometimes the agent follows *de. De* is used for mental or emotional reactions (less action than response):

*Sus obras **eran reconocidas de** todo el mundo.* → His works were recognized by everyone.

De is also used when neither *ser* nor *estar* is expressed:

*Este maestro, **venerado de** todos los estudiantes . . .* → This teacher, admired by all the students . . .

Time	Active	Passive
Present	María agarra la pelota.	La pelota **es agarrada por** María.
Present Perfect	El hombre ha leído los libros.	Los libros **han sido leídos por** el hombre.

All other tenses are formed by using the appropriate tense of *ser* (or *estar*) plus the past participle of the verb in question.

WHAT USES DOES IT HAVE? Speakers of Spanish believe that the passive is a weak voice and that the active voice is preferable.

Sometimes we tend to use less vivid language when using the passive. Compare the following sentences:

PASSIVE	**ACTIVE**
Our receiver was tackled by their defensive end.	Their defensive end slammed our receiver to the ground.
This abstract was painted by Pablo Picasso.	Pablo Picasso created this colorful abstract.

Sometimes, when we do not know who the agent was, or when we are more interested in the result than the action, the passive is sufficient.

*La casa **está destruida.*** → The house is destroyed.
*El poema **fue escrito** por Bécquer.* → The poem was written by Bécquer.

For the most part, though, it is better to use the active voice. In Spanish there are a number of good ways to avoid using the passive:

1. Turn the sentence around:

    Not: *El libro **fue leído por** la clase.*   **But:** *La clase **leyó** el libro.*

2. Use an impersonal construction:

    Not: *Aquí el español **es hablado.***   **But:** ***Se habla** español.*

3. Use the reflexive:

    Not: *Ayer los vestidos **eran vendidos** a bajo precio.*   **But:** ***Ayer** los vestidos **se vendían** a bajo precio.*

Imperative Mood in English

WHAT IS IT? The **imperative mood** is the command mood.

WHAT FORMS DOES IT HAVE? The forms of the imperative are very similar to those of the present indicative with a few exceptions. The imperative exists in only one form:

Second person (singular and plural the same): *Sing!*

For the first person plural and the third persons, one of the auxiliary verbs *let, have,* or *make* is used:

First person plural: *Let's (let us) sing!*
Third persons: *Let him (them) sing! Have them come in! Make him stop!*

NOTE: No subject is expressed for the imperative.

Irregular imperatives. There is only one irregular imperative in English: the verb *to be*.

Compare:

Indicative	Imperative
You are good.	Be good!
We are quiet.	Let's be quiet!

VERBS 113

Imperative Mood in Spanish

WHAT FORMS DOES IT HAVE? Only affirmative *tú* and *vosotros* commands have special forms for the imperative. The *tú* form drops the "-s" of the indicative. The *vosotros* form is the same as the infinitive, except that a "-d" replaces the "r."

All other forms, including the third person and the *tú* and *vosotros* forms in negative commands, use the present subjunctive form for a command (see p. 115):

Affirmative Commands

Person	Hablar	Comer	Vivir
tú	¡habla!	¡come!	¡vive!
vosotros/as	¡hablad!	¡comed!	¡vivid!
nosotros/as	¡hablemos!	¡comamos!	¡vivamos!
usted	¡hable!	¡coma!	¡viva!
ustedes	¡hablen!	¡coman!	¡vivan!

Negative Commands

Person	Hablar	Comer	Vivir
tú	¡no hables!	¡no comas!	¡no vivas!
vosotros/as	¡no habléis!	¡no comáis!	¡no viváis!

As you would expect, to form a negative command, you simply place *no* before the affirmative command for the *nosotros/as, usted* and *ustedes* forms also.

Irregular imperatives. Some verbs have irregular forms in the imperative mood:

Verb:	tú	vosotros/as	usted	nosotros/as	ustedes
decir	di	decid	diga	digamos	digan
hacer	haz	haced	haga	hagamos	hagan
ir	ve	id	vaya	vayamos	vayan

WORD ORDER. In *affirmative* commands, pronoun subjects, if expressed, follow the verb:

Hablen (ustedes) español. Ven (tú) conmigo.

The object(s), if any, are attached to the verb (see p. 30):

¡Dígame! ¡Escríbalo! ¡Vámonos!

In *negative* commands, the objects return to their normal position and order.

¡No me diga! ¡No lo escriba! ¡No nos vayamos!

Subjunctive Mood in English

WHAT IS IT? The **subjunctive** is the mood that expresses what *may* be true.

WHAT FORMS DOES IT HAVE? The subjunctive does not change for persons. The **present subjunctive** form of the verb (or the auxiliary verb in a compound tense) is always the same: the basic, or infinitive form, of the verb. Therefore, it is different from the indicative only for:

1. the third person singular:

   that he take, that he have, etc.

2. the verb *to be:*

   Present

   that I be, that he be, etc.

   Past

   that I were, that she were, etc.

WHAT USES DOES IT HAVE? The subjunctive is used only infrequently in English. For that reason, we tend to forget about it except in certain fixed expressions. Nevertheless, it does have some specific uses that are important in formal English:

1. Contrary-to-fact conditions:

   *If I **were** you . . .*   *"If this **be** madness, yet there is method in it."* (Hamlet)

2. After verbs such as *wish, suppose, insist, urge, demand, ask, recommend,* and *suggest:*

   *I wish that he **were** able to come.*   *They insisted that we **be** present.*

   *I recommend that he **learn** the subjunctive.*

3. After some impersonal expressions, such as *it is necessary,* and *it is important:*

   *It is important that he **avoid** errors.*   *It is necessary that Mary **see** its use.*

4. In some fixed expressions:

   *So **be** it!   Long **live** the Queen!   Heaven **forbid**!*
   *Far **be** it from me to suggest that!*

NOTE: Most of the fixed expressions are a way of expressing a third person imperative. The idea, "I wish that" is implied, but not expressed.

Whenever possible (except for the fixed expressions), we tend to use an alternate expression, usually with modals (auxiliaries), in order to avoid the subjunctive in conversation and informal writing. Compare these sentences with the examples above:

*I wish that he **could come**.*
*I told her that she **must learn** the subjunctive.*
*It is important for him **to avoid** errors.*
*Mary **needs to see** its importance.*

Subjunctive Mood in Spanish

WHAT FORMS DOES IT HAVE? The **subjunctive mood** has four commonly used tenses in Spanish: present, imperfect, present perfect, and pluperfect (past perfect). The present subjunctive is formed by dropping the "-o" of the first person singular to form the stem, and then adding the appropriate endings from the chart below.

Stem-changing verbs like *pensar, volver, pedir,* etc. will have the stem change in the subjunctive because it is present in the *yo* form. Verbs that end in "-car" or "-gar" will change the "c" to "qu" and the "g" to "gu" before an "e" in the subjunctive, exactly as they did in the indicative: *tocar/toque; pagar/pague.*

The dominant vowel of the "-ar" verbs becomes "e," while the dominant vowel of both the "-er" and "-ir" verbs becomes "a:"

Hablar	**Comer**	**Abrir**
(yo hablo)	*(yo como)*	*(yo abro)*
hable	coma	abra
hables	comas	abras
hable	coma	abra
hablemos	comamos	abramos
habléis	comáis	abráis
hablen	coman	abran

NOTE: Remember that there are several verbs in Spanish whose *yo* form ends in *-go:*

distingo (distinguir); pongo (poner); sigo (seguir); salgo (salir); hago (hacer); digo (decir); tengo (tener); and *oigo (oír)*

Also remember that some verbs, like *seguir,* are stem-changing and drop the "u" of the infinitive to reflect the "hard sound:" *sigo/siga.* Others simply have an irregular *yo* form in the present indicative: *conozco/conozca; venzo/venza; escojo/escoja.*

Irregular present subjunctives. Some common verbs are irregular in the present subjunctive:

Infinitive	Irregular Stem Plus Endings
haber	haya, etc.
ser	sea, etc.
ir	vaya, etc.
estar	esté, estés, esté, estemos, estéis, estén
dar	dé, des, dé, demos, deis, den
saber	sepa, etc.
ver	vea, etc.

(Continued on p. 116)

Subjunctive Mood
in Spanish
(continued)

WHAT USES DOES IT HAVE? In theory the subjunctive is used to show that what is being said is:

1. potentially (but not actually) true.

2. colored by emotion (which often distorts facts).

3. expressing your attitude toward something (rather than the actual facts).

4. doubtful, probably nonexistent, or not true.

In *practice* there are certain words and expressions that require the subjunctive. The theory may help you remember which ones they are, but you cannot argue theory against practice. If an expression requires the subjunctive, then it must be used whether or not you believe that it fits well into the theoretical bases.

The subjunctive is used principally:

1. after verbs or other expressions conveying the subject's emotional reactions:

   Estoy contento que . . .   *Tememos que . . .*   *Me sorprende que . . .*

2. after verbs such as *querer* and *exigir* when there is a change of subject:

   Subjunctive: *Quiero que Raúl venga.* (Note change of subject.)

   Infinitive: *Quiero venir.* (no change of subject)

3. after verbs of doubt, negation, necessity, importance, and opinion when uncertainty is conveyed. Contrast the following lists:

Subjunctive	Indicative
Dudo que mi padre **venga**.	**Estoy cierto** que mi madre **viene**.
Niega que este hombre **sea** su padre.	**Es verdad** que este hombre **es** su padre.
Es posible que yo no **venga**.	
Es increíble que él no me **crea**.	**Es seguro** que él me **cree**.
Ojalá que **venga**.	**Es cierto** que **viene**.
Es bueno que tú no **tengas** hambre.	
Es importante que ustedes **aprendan** el español.	

4. after conjunctions expressing:

concession:	*aunque; bien que*
purpose:	*por que; a fin de que*
indefinite time:	*hasta que; antes de que*
negation:	*sin que; a menos que*

5. after superlatives (because of possible emotional exaggeration). Contrast the following statements:

   Es el mejor poema que **conozca.** → It's the best poem I know. (Meaning: I really like it!)

   Es el joven más alto que yo **conozco.** → He's the tallest young man I know. (Meaning: None of my other friends are so tall.)

The first statement conveys an emotion. The second states a fact. The indicative and subjunctive respectively tell your audience how you mean the statement. Some Spanish-speakers do not make this distinction and use the subjunctive in all cases.

(Continued on p. 117)

6. After relative pronouns referring to an indefinite antecedent:

*Quiero hablar con **alguien que conozca** bien la ciudad.*

7. Some verbs (especially *pensar* and *creer*) take the subjunctive in the negative or interrogative, because asking what someone thinks, or saying what someone does not believe, implies doubt about the true situation. The negative-interrogative often takes the indicative because you expect a positive response:

*¿Cree Ud. que el profesor **esté** enfermo?*
*No creo que el profesor **esté** enfermo.*
*¿No cree Ud. que el profesor **esté** (or **está**) enfermo?*

8. For third person commands:

*¡Que **se callen**!* → Let them be quiet! (contrast Imperative Mood, p. 113).

9. In certain fixed expressions:

*¡**Viva** el Rey!* → Long live the King!

To remember the principal uses of the subjunctive, think of **NEEDS PAWS:**

Necessity
Emotion
Exaggeration
Demanding
Seeming

Possibility
Asking
Wishing
Supposing

The Imperfect Subjunctive

WHAT FORMS DOES IT HAVE? The **imperfect subjunctive** is formed by first dropping the *-ron* ending of the third person plural preterite to form the stem for all regular and irregular verbs. There are two sets of endings:

Form I

Estudiar	Comer	Abrir	Decir
estudiara	comiera	abriera	dijera
estudiaras	comieras	abrieras	dijeras
estudiara	comiera	abriera	dijera
estudiáramos	comiéramos	abriéramos	dijéramos
estudiarais	comierais	abrierais	dijerais
estudiaran	comieran	abrieran	dijeran

Note that the *nosotros* form takes an accent.

(Continued on p. 118)

Form II

Estudiar	Comer	Abrir	Decir
estudiase	comiese	abriese	dijese
estudiases	comieses	abrieses	dijeses
estudiase	comiese	abriese	dijese
estudiásemos	comiésemos	abriésemos	dijésemos
estudiaseis	comieseis	abrieseis	dijeseis
estudiasen	comiesen	abriesen	dijesen

While there are two forms of the imperfect subjunctive, generally Form 1 is used more commonly in speech; Form II is generally limited to formal writing in most Spanish-speaking cultures, and is often used in everyday speech in Spain. It can be replaced by Form I, but you should be able to recognize it.

While a future subjunctive exists in Spanish, it is rarely used and will not be introduced here.

There is no conditional subjunctive in Spanish; the imperfect subjunctive is used where a conditional idea is expressed.

WHAT USES DOES IT HAVE? The imperfect subjunctive appears in subordinate clauses when:

1. the verb in the main clause requiring a subjunctive is in the past:

   *Los estudiantes **temían** que el profesor **estuviera** enfermo.* → The students were afraid that the professor was sick.

2. the verb in the main clause that requires a subjunctive is in the present indicative, but the idea expressed by the subordinate clause is a past tense:

   ***Es bueno** que él **llegara** ayer.* → It's good that he arrived yesterday.

The Present Perfect Subjunctive

WHAT FORMS DOES IT HAVE? The **present perfect subjunctive** is formed by the present subjunctive of the auxiliary verb *haber* plus the past participle of the main verb:

Auxiliary	Past Participle
haya	hablado
hayas	perdido
haya	salido
hayamos	dicho
hayáis	visto
hayan	estado

(Continued on p. 119)

The Past Subjunctive (continued)

WHAT USES DOES IT HAVE? The present perfect subjunctive is found in subordinate clauses that express an action that has taken place or may have taken place when that verb is governed by a verbal or other expression that requires a subjunctive:

Espero que el profesor haya leído nuestros exámenes. → I hope the professor has read our exams.

Aunque el profesor haya leído los exámenes, eso no significa que hoy él va a devolvérselos a los estudiantes. → Although the professor may have read the exams, that doesn't mean that he's going to return them to the students today.

Cuando usted haya decidido, dígamelo por favor. → When you have decided, please tell me.

Pluperfect (Past Perfect) Subjunctive

WHAT FORMS DOES IT HAVE? Like the imperfect subjunctive, the **pluperfect (past perfect) subjunctive** has two forms. The tense is formed with the imperfect subjunctive of the auxiliary verb *haber* and the past participle of the verb:

Form I

Auxiliary	Past Participle
hubiera	estudiado
hubieras	comido
hubiera	vivido
hubiéramos	abierto
hubierais	dicho
hubieran	visto

Form II

Auxiliary	Past Participle
hubiese	estudiado
hubieses	comido
hubiese	vivido
hubiésemos	salido
hubieseis	dicho
hubiesen	visto

WHAT USES DOES IT HAVE? The past perfect subjunctive appears in subordinate clauses in which the action has occurred prior to the action of the verb in the main clause:

Temían que Alicia hubiera partido. → They were afraid that Alice had left.

No creí que Ramón hubiera mentido. → I did not believe that Raymond had lied (or would have lied).

Yo no habría creído que el profesor hubiera podido hacer lo que había hecho. → I would not have believed that the professor could have done what he had done.

Exercises

The following exercises, grouped by part of speech, test your grasp of key grammatical aspects of Spanish. For help and a reminder of the similarities and differences between Spanish and English in each area, a cross-reference is provided at the foot of the exercise to the relevant section of the book. An answer key is provided after the Appendices.

Nouns and Determiners

A *Add the correct definite article to each of the following Spanish nouns.*

1. _____ clase

2. _____ libro

3. _____ azúcar

4. _____ agua

5. _____ aguas

6. _____ padres

7. _____ coches

8. _____ guerra

9. _____ lápiz

10. _____ mesa

▶ *For more help, see* Determiners, *pp. 20–22.*

B *Add the correct indefinite article to each of the following Spanish nouns.*

1. _____ casa

2. _____ pared

3. _____ ventanas

4. _____ suelo

5. _____ techo

6. _____ habitaciones

7. _____ escalera

8. _____ sótano

9. _____ cocina

10. _____ muebles

▶ *For more help, see* Determiners, *pp. 20–22.*

C   *Complete the following sentences with the correct form of the definite or indefinite article.*

1. ¿Hay _____ restaurantes por aquí?

2. Sí, _____ restaurantes de este barrio son muy buenos.

3. ¿_____ comida es cara en esos restaurantes?

4. _____ restaurantes son caros, otros no.

5. ¿Hay _____ restaurante mexicano en el barrio?

6. Oh, sí. _____ restaurante mexicano es uno de mis restaurantes favoritos.

7. _____ platos que sirven son auténticos y muy variados.

8. Me gustaría comer _____ enchiladas.

9. En ese caso, vamos allí ahora. _____ enchiladas que sirven son las mejores que he probado.

10. Y yo voy a pedir _____ tacos también.

▶ *For more help, see* Determiners, *pp. 20–22.*

Pronouns

A   *What subject pronouns can go with these present-tense verb forms? List all possibilities.*

1. hablamos   _____

2. escribo   _____

3. vende   _____

4. estáis   _____

5. bailan   _____

6. es   _____

7. puedo   _____

8. eres _____

9. vivís _____

10. ponen _____

11. comes _____

12. hacemos _____

▶ *For more help, see* Personal Pronouns, *p. 27.*

B *Rewrite each of the following sentences, replacing the italicized direct object noun by the corresponding direct object pronoun.*

1. Tenemos *los disquetes.* _____

2. Preparan *la cena.* _____

3. Reparo *las computadoras.* _____

4. ¿No bebes *el jugo?* _____

5. No conocen *a María Elena.* _____

6. Ya leí *las revistas.* _____

7. Llevamos *a los niños* al zoológico. _____

8. ¿Compraron Uds. *los regalos?* _____

9. Vendieron *su coche.* _____

10. El niño rompió *el juguete.* _____

▶ *For more help, see* Personal Pronouns, *pp. 26–27.*

C *Rewrite each of the following sentences, replacing the italicized direct object noun by the corresponding direct object pronoun. The sentences with infinitives have two possibilities each.*

1. Haz *el café.* _____

2. No sirvas *los pasteles.* _____

3. Quiero comer *la torta.* _____

   _____

4. ¿Debo cerrar *la puerta?* _____

   _____

5. Pongan *los libros* en la mesa. _____

6. Abra *las ventanas.* _____

7. ¿Podemos ver *las fotos*? _____

_____

8. Los estudiantes piensan estudiar *el texto*.

_____

_____

9. ¿Puede Ud. traducir *este mensaje*? _____

_____

10. Saca *la basura*. _____

▶ *For more help, see* Personal Pronouns, *pp. 26–29.*

D   *Complete each of the following exchanges with the missing direct object pronoun.*

1. Sr. Gómez: ¿Ud. me conoce, señora?

   Sra. López: No, señor. No _____ conozco.

2. Amalia: ¿Pablo te va a invitar?

   Carla: No sé si va a invitar_____.

3. Abuela: ¿El tío Francisco les escribe?

   Niños: Sí, _____ escribe todas las semanas.

4. Carlos: ¿Te molesto?

   Liliana: No, no _____ molestas.

5. Federico: ¿Sabes si Lucas desea hablar conmigo?

   Ana: Sí, creo que _____ busca.

▶ *For more help, see* Personal Pronouns, *pp. 26–29.*

E   *Rewrite the following sentences, replacing the italicized words by the correct direct and indirect object pronouns. The sentences will have two object pronouns.*

1. Les envían *los regalos a sus padres*. _____

2. Le lee *el cuento a su hija*. _____

3. Dales *los juguetes a los niños*. _____

4. Les mando *el dinero a mis primos*. _____

5. ¿Puedes devolverme *los cien dólares*? _____

6. Les enseña *el español a los estudiantes.* _____

7. Te voy a mostrar *las fotos.* _____

8. A Ud. le voy a vender *mi coche.* _____

9. Me pongo *el abrigo.* _____

10. Dígame *la verdad.* _____

11. Voy a prepararte *el café.* _____

12. ¿Les explicas *la lección a tus amigos*? _____

▶ *For more help, see* Personal Pronouns, *pp. 27–30.*

F *Complete the following sentences with the missing disjunctive pronoun.*

1. A _____ no nos gusta este barrio.

2. ¿Y a _____ qué te gusta comer?

3. A _____ me gustan mucho los tacos.

4. Este regalo es para _____, señora. Espero que le guste.

5. Uds. no lo invitaron a la fiesta. Por eso él está enojado con _____.

6. Tú nunca piensas en _____. Nunca me llamas, nunca me vienes a ver.

▶ *For more help, see* Pronouns as Objects of Prepositions, *pp. 28–29, and* Disjunctive Pronouns, *p. 35.*

G *Complete the following sentences with the missing possessive pronoun so that the Spanish matches the English.*

1. I like my bicycle, but he prefers his.

   A mí me gusta la bicicleta mía, pero él prefiere _____.

2. This house is older than ours.

   Esta casa es más antigua que _____.

3. These books aren't María's, they're mine.

   Estos libros no son los de María, son _____.

4. I have my notes. Do you have yours?

   Yo tengo mis notas. ¿Tienes _____?

5. She needs my pencil because she has lost hers.

   Ella necesita el lápiz mío porque ha perdido _____.

6. My car is broken down. Can you take yours?

   Tengo el coche descompuesto. ¿Puede Ud. llevar _____?

7. I brought my photos, and they brought theirs.

   Yo traje las fotos mías y ellos trajeron _____.

8. Our dog is bigger than theirs.

   Nuestro perro es más grande que _____.

9. I like your class. It's better than mine.

   Me gusta tu clase. Es mejor que _____.

10. I forgot my diskettes. Could you lend me yours?

    Se me olvidaron mis disquetes. ¿Podría Ud. prestarme _____?

11. I think my report is longer than yours.

    Creo que el informe mío es más largo que _____.

12. First we'll go to his house and then to mine.

    Primero iremos a la casa de él y después a _____.

▶ *For more help, see* Possessive Pronouns, *pp. 30–31.*

H *Select the correct relative pronoun to complete each of the following sentences.*

1. Aquí tienes el artículo _____ he leído.
   a. que
   b. quien
   c. quienes
   d. lo que
   e. cuyo

2. Voy a presentarte al colega con _____ yo trabajaba antes.
   a. que
   b. quien
   c. quienes
   d. lo que
   e. cuyo

3. Éstos son los niños para _____ he comprado los juguetes.
   a. que
   b. quien
   c. quienes
   d. lo que
   e. cuyo

4. No comprendemos _____ quieres.
    a. que
    b. quien
    c. quienes
    d. lo que
    e. cuyo

5. Ésta es la señora _____ trabaja aquí.
    a. que
    b. quien
    c. quienes
    d. lo que
    e. cuyo

6. Eso es _____ me sorprendió.
    a. que
    b. quien
    c. quienes
    d. lo que
    e. cuyo

7. El escritor _____ libro leí es muy famoso.
    a. que
    b. quien
    c. quienes
    d. lo que
    e. cuyo

8. El ingeniero de _____ Ud. me habló es muy inteligente.
    a. que
    b. quien
    c. quienes
    d. lo que
    e. cuyo

▶ *For more help, see* Relative Pronouns, *pp. 36–39.*

I *Translate the following sentences into Spanish using demonstrative pronouns.*

1. This book and that one *(near you)*. _____

2. These houses and those *(over there)*. _____

3. These restaurants are good, but those *(over there)* are better.

    _____

4. That *(near you)* cell phone (**teléfono celular**) is good, but this one is excellent.

    _____

5. I like cars, but I don't like that one *(over there)*.

    _____

6. These gardens and those *(near you)* have beautiful flowers.

_____

7. Do you *(tú)* want those *(over there)* pastries or these?

_____

8. That bicycle *(near you)* is more expensive than this one.

_____

▶ *For more help, see* Demonstrative Pronouns, *pp. 40–41.*

J *Complete each of the following Spanish sentences with the missing interrogative pronoun so that they match the English sentences in meaning.*

1. Whom are you writing to?

¿_____ le escribes?

2. What are you looking for?

¿_____ buscan Uds.?

3. Whom *(which people)* did you invite?

¿_____ invitaste?

4. I like these two cars. Which is less expensive?

Me gustan estos dos coches. ¿_____ es menos caro?

5. What is the child afraid of?

¿_____ tiene miedo el niño?

6. Whom is she going out with?

¿_____ sale ella?

7. What are you thinking about?

¿_____ piensas tú?

8. There are so many newspapers. How many do you read?

Hay tantos periódicos. ¿_____ lee Ud.?

9. Who works there?

¿_____ trabaja allí?

10. What have you done?

¿_____ has hecho?

11. Whom did you see?

    ¿_____ has visto?

12. How much sugar do you need?

    ¿_____ azúcar necesitas?

13. Whom (*which people*) are these gifts for?

    ¿_____ son estos regalos?

14. Here are several computers. Which ones do you prefer?

    Aquí hay varias computadoras. ¿_____ prefieres?

▶ *For more help, see* Interrogative Pronouns, *pp. 42–43.*

Adjectives

A *Complete the following lists with the missing forms of the adjective.*

1. a. un libro _____

   b. una historia _____

   c. libros interesantes

   d. historias _____

2. a. un árbol blanco

   b. una flor _____

   c. árboles _____

   d. flores _____

3. a. un hombre _____

   b. una mujer _____

   c. unos hombres españoles

   d. unas mujeres _____

4. a. un pueblo andaluz

   b. una ciudad _____

   c. pueblos _____

   d. ciudades _____

5. a. un _____ libro

   b. una _____ revista

   c. buenos <u>libros</u>

   d. _____ revistas

6. a. un muchacho _____

   b. una muchacha <u>joven</u>

   c. unos muchachos _____

   d. unas muchachas _____

7. a. un examen <u>fácil</u>

   b. una tarea _____

   c. unos exámenes _____

   d. unas tareas _____

8. a. _____ monumento

   b. _____ estatua

   c. algunos <u>monumentos</u>

   d. _____ estatuas

9. a. un restaurante _____

   b. una cerveza _____

   c. restaurantes _____

   d. cervezas <u>alemanas</u>

10. a. un _____ profesor

    b. una _____ profesora

    c. _____ profesores

    d. grandes <u>profesoras</u>

▶ *For more help, see* Adjectives, *pp. 48–49.*

B   *Complete the following phrases according to the English cue in parentheses.*

1. (third) el _____ día

2. (no) _____ posibilidad

3. (bad) un _____ momento

4. (first) mi _____ idea

5. (some) _____ acontecimiento

6. (great) un _____ científico

7. (third) la _____ parada

8. (no) _____ curso

9. (first) su _____ viaje

10. (good) un _____ amigo

▶ *For more help, see* Adjectives, *pp. 48–49.*

C   *Put the correct form of **Santo** before each of these names.*

1. _____ José

2. _____ Ana

3. _____ Tomás

4. _____ Lucía

5. _____ Pedro

6. _____ María

7. _____ Domingo

8. _____ Lucas

9. _____ Bárbara

10. _____ Antonio

▶ *For more help, see* Adjectives, *pp. 48–49.*

D   *Translate the following phrases into Spanish.*

1. a poor (unfortunate) man _____

2. a friend of many years *(fem.)* _____

3. a former general _____

4. an ancient city _____

5. a great woman _____

6. a poor (penniless) man _____

7. a tall girl _____

8. an elderly neighbor *(masc.)* _____

▶ *For more help, see* Adjectives, *pp. 48–49.*

E   *Translate the following sentences into Spanish.*

1. Jaime is more intelligent than Raúl.

   _____

2. My sister is less studious *(**aplicada**)* than my brother.

   _____

3. It's the best book in the library.

   _____

4. The subway is faster than the bus.

   _____

5. He is the worst student at the school.

   _____

6. My course is less interesting than their course.

   _____

▶ *For more help, see* Comparison of Adjectives, *pp. 50–51.*

F *Translate the following phrases into Spanish. Each one contains a demonstrative adjective.*

1. those women *(over there)* _____

2. this book _____

3. that table _____

4. those planes _____

5. that car *(over there)* _____

6. these chairs _____

7. those windows _____

8. that door *(over there)* _____

9. this page _____

10. those buses *(over there)* _____

11. those trains _____

12. these exams _____

▶ *For more help, see* Demonstrative Adjectives, *pp. 54–55.*

G *Translate the following phrases into Spanish.*

1. her book _____

2. my school _____

3. his house _____

4. our translation _____

5. their gardens _____

6. your *(fam. sing.)* ideas _____

7. your *(**Uds.**)* notebooks _____

8. my homework assignments _____

9. your *(fam.)* composition _____

10. his story _____

▶ *For more help, see* Possessive Adjectives, *pp. 56–57.*

Adverbs

A   *Write the adverb that corresponds to each of the following adjectives.*

1. fácil   _____

2. nervioso   _____

3. maravilloso _____

4. bueno   _____

5. lento   _____

6. claro   _____

7. natural   _____

8. cuidadoso   _____

9. responsable _____

10. feroz   _____

▶ *For more help, see* Adverbs, *pp. 62–63.*

B   *Write the following negative sentences in Spanish.*

1. He doesn't work. _____

2. He doesn't work anymore. _____

3. He never works. _____

4. No one works. _____

5. She is not learning anything. _____

6. We don't see Paula or Carmen. _____

▶ *For more help, see* Adverbs, *pp. 64–65.*

Prepositions

A *Complete the following sentences with the Spanish equivalent of the preposition in parentheses.*

1. (to) Ella va _____ España.

2. (near) Vivimos _____ la plaza.

3. (in) Trabajan _____ México.

4. (in front of) Hay un jardín _____ mi casa.

5. (under) Están sentados _____ un árbol.

6. (before) Vinieron _____ las tres.

▶ *For more help, see* Prepositions, *pp. 76–77.*

B *Supply the correct preposition before the infinitive. If no preposition is required, put an* X.

1. Él está aquí. Acabo _____ verlo.

2. Voy _____ buscarlo, entonces.

3. Mi habitación da _____ la calle.

4. No sé si puedo _____ ir.

5. Llegaron _____ respetarlo.

6. Lo vi cuando miré _____ la ventana.

7. No te pongas _____ llorar.

8. Trato _____ comprenderlo.

9. Vino _____ decirme que no podía ir.

10. ¿Qué quieres _____ hacer?

11. ¿Por qué se ríen Uds. _____ mí?

12. Hoy empecé _____ estudiar para el examen.

▶ *For more help, see* Prepositions, *p. 78.*

Verbs

A *Complete the following chart with the present and past participles of the infinitives given.*

INFINITIVE	PRESENT PARTICIPLE	PAST PARTICIPLE
1. decir	_____	_____
2. ir	_____	_____
3. ver	_____	_____
4. morir	_____	_____
5. abrir	_____	_____
6. poner	_____	_____
7. sentir	_____	_____
8. dormir	_____	_____
9. escribir	_____	_____
10. romper	_____	_____
11. hacer	_____	_____
12. volver	_____	_____

▶ *For more help, see* Participles, *pp. 86–87.*

B *Give the present tense form of the verb in parentheses.*

1. (caminar) Los muchachos _____ rápidamente.

2. (aprender) Yo _____ mucho en esta clase.

3. (entender) ¿_____ (tú) lo que te dicen?

4. (pensar) Ellos _____ irse de vacaciones.

5. (sentir) ¿Te molesté? ¡Cuánto lo _____!

6. (mostrar) ¿Por qué no me _____ (tú) tus fotos?

7. (jugar) Los niños _____ en el parque.

8. (pedir) Él siempre me _____ ayuda.

9. (repetir) Ella siempre _____ la misma cosa.

10. (permitir) Nosotros no te lo _____.

11. (comer) Hoy (nosotros) _____ en el centro.

12. (seguir) Yo _____ en la misma clase.

13. (hacer) ¿Qué _____ yo ahora?

14. (traer) Espera y yo te lo _____.

15. (estar) Yo no _____ enojado.

▶ *For more help, see* Present Tense, *pp. 90–91 and 93.*

C   *Write the equivalent present progressive form for each of the following present tense forms.*

1. trabaja   _____

2. vuelvo   _____

3. escribes   _____

4. camina   _____

5. pedimos   _____

6. duermen   _____

7. oigo   _____

8. mientes   _____

▶ *For more help, see* Present Progressive, *pp. 90–91.*

D   *Rewrite the following sentences in the imperfect.*

1. Habla con su novia. _____

2. Terminamos nuestro trabajo. _____

3. Ella hace un café. _____

4. Espero a mis amigos. _____

5. El niño duerme. _____

6. Estamos preocupados. _____

7. Vendes tu casa. _____

8. Ella trabaja en esta oficina. _____

9. Estudiamos nuestras lecciones. _____

10. Siguen por esta calle. _____

11. Van al centro. _____

12. Veo películas en la tele. _____

13. Escribes una carta. _____

14. Ud. lee mucho. _____

15. Salgo. _____

16. Ella está en el centro. _____

17. Es inteligente. _____

18. Nunca pierdes nada. _____

▶ *For more help, see* Imperfect, *pp. 93–94.*

E *Write the equivalent imperfect progressive form for each of the following imperfect tense forms.*

1. comían   _____

2. veías   _____

3. éramos   _____

4. yo hablaba   _____

5. salíamos   _____

6. regresaban   _____

7. ella llegaba   _____

8. vivías   _____

▶ *For more help, see* Imperfect Progressive, *p. 94.*

F *Complete the following sentences with the preterite of the verb in parentheses.*

1. (comprar) Nosotros no _____ nada en el centro.

2. (prender) ¿(Tú) _____ la tele?

3. (buscar) Lo _____ pero no lo encontré.

4. (tener) Yo _____ que salir.

5. (sentirse) Ella _____ mal.

6. (dormir) ¿Ud. no _____ bien?

7. (escribir) ¿(Tú) _____ la carta?

8. (empezar) Yo _____ a estudiar anoche.

9. (poner) ¿Qué _____ Juan en la mochila?

10. (hacer) ¿Qué _____ Sonia ayer?

11. (decir) Ellos no me _____ nada.

12. (traducir) ¿Quién _____ el mensaje?

13. (venir) ¿A qué hora _____ tus amigos?

14. (ser) El verano _____ bueno.

15. (saber) ¿Cuándo _____ tú que él no iba a venir?

16. (querer) Me invitaron, pero no _____ ir.

17. (dar) Yo no me _____ cuenta de nada.

18. (pagar) Yo _____ la cuenta.

19. (comer) Nosotros _____ en casa ayer.

20. (dar) ¿Qué regalos te _____ tus abuelos?

21. (estar) ¡Qué rico _____ la comida!

22. (caminar) Ellos _____ una hora.

23. (ir) ¿(Tú) _____ en avión?

24. (poder) Queríamos ir, pero no _____.

▶ *For more help, see* Preterite, *p. 95.*

G *Answer each of the following questions with* **No sé si** + *future tense. Follow the model.*

MODELO   ¿Juan va a terminar?   No sé si terminará.

1. ¿Ellos van a salir? _____

2. ¿Voy a poder? _____

3. ¿Nuestro equipo va a perder? _____

4. ¿Vas a hacerlo? _____

5. ¿Uds. van a saberlo? _____

6. ¿Lo vas a decir? _____

7. ¿Ud. va a abrir la puerta? _____

8. ¿Uds. van a poner la mesa? _____

9. ¿Va a haber una reunión? _____

10. ¿Voy a querer? _____

▶ *For more help, see* Future Tense, *pp. 96–97.*

H   *Complete the following sentences with the correct form of the conditional of the verb in parentheses.*

1. (tener) Yo creía que los niños _____ hambre.

2. (poner) Si pudiera escoger, me _____ la otra corbata.

3. (echar) Ella sabía que nosotros _____ la carta al correo.

4. (hacer) Estos chicos _____ su trabajo si comprendieran la tarea.

5. (escribir) Yo creía que Uds. me _____ más mensajes electrónicos.

6. (salir) Sabíamos que tú _____ con nosotros.

7. (caber) Pensábamos que la maleta _____.

8. (decir) Yo te _____ la respuesta si la supiera.

9. (vender) Si pudiéramos, _____ nuestra casa.

10. (querer) Ella nos dijo que tú _____ ir.

11. (haber) Yo no sabía si _____ una fiesta o no.

12. (dar) En ese caso yo no le _____ el dinero.

▶ *For more help, see* Conditional, *pp. 98–99.*

I   *Use the present perfect to say that all these things have already been done. Follow the model.*

MODELO   ¿Carmela va a salir?   <u>Ya ha salido.</u>

1. ¿Vas a abrir las ventanas? _____

2. ¿Los chicos van a poner la mesa? _____

3. ¿Uds. van a hacer ejercicio? _____

4. ¿José va a llamar? _____

5. ¿Vas a pedir una pizza? _____

6. ¿Nosotros vamos a ver la película? _____

7. ¿Carlos y Pedro van a volver? _____

8. ¿Van Uds. a escribir el mensaje? _____

▶ *For more help, see* Present Perfect, *pp. 100–101.*

J *Answer each of these questions in the past perfect (pluperfect) using the word **ya** as in the model.*

MODELO ¿Ella quería cenar? ___Ya había cenado.___

1. ¿Tu mamá quería salir? _____

2. ¿Tú querías hacer el té? _____

3. ¿Los niños querían jugar? _____

4. ¿Ellas querían volver? _____

5. ¿Uds. querían hablar? _____

6. ¿Querías telefonear? _____

7. ¿Ellos querían verlo? _____

8. Uds. querían comer? _____

▶ *For more help, see* Past Perfect, *pp. 104–105.*

K *Use the future perfect tense to express surprise at each of these events. Follow the model.*

MODELO ¡Se escapó el gato! ___¿Cómo se habrá escapado?___

1. ¡Ellos lo supieron! _____

2. ¡Tú ganaste! _____

3. ¡Los amigos llegaron! _____

4. ¡Uds. sacaron el premio! _____

5. ¡Yo conseguí el trabajo! _____

6. ¡El niño reparó el juguete! _____

▶ *For more help, see* Future Perfect, *pp. 106–107.*

L *Rewrite the following sentences in the passive. Keep the same tense as in the original sentence.*

1. Los niños tiran la pelota.

_____

2. Pablo escribió el mensaje.

_____

3. Los expertos han estudiado el informe.

_____

4. Todos admiran a esta cantante.

    _____

5. La policía arrestó a los criminales.

    _____

6. Mi abuela ha hecho la cena.

    _____

7. La ciudad construirá un nuevo estadio.

    _____

8. El director organizará un comité.

    _____

▶ *For more help, see* Passive Voice, *pp. 110–111.*

M *Fill out the following chart with informal singular commands. The first answers are given as a model.*

INFINITIVE	AFFIRMATIVE COMMAND	NEGATIVE COMMAND
1. llamarlo	Llámalo.	No lo llames.
2. dármelo		
3. escribirle		
4. salir		
5. decírnoslo		
6. hacerlo		
7. vendérsela		
8. ponerlo		

▶ *For more help, see* Imperative, *pp. 112–113.*

N *Fill out the following chart with formal singular commands. The first answers are given as a model.*

INFINITIVE	AFFIRMATIVE COMMAND	NEGATIVE COMMAND
1. llamarlo	Llámelo.	No lo llame.
2. decírmelo		
3. abrirlas		

4. oírla

    _____   _____

5. verlos

    _____   _____

6. hacerlo

    _____   _____

7. aprenderlos

    _____   _____

8. conocerlo

    _____   _____

▶ *For more help, see* Imperative, *pp. 112–113.*

O   *Complete the following sentences with the present subjunctive or the present indicative of the verb in parentheses.*

1. (poder) Es poco probable que él _____ venir.

2. (entender) No creo que ella _____ lo que le dices.

3. (querer) Sé que los chicos _____ acompañarnos.

4. (saber) Me sorprende que tú no _____ la respuesta.

5. (escoger) Él teme que yo no lo _____.

6. (ir) Estamos contentos que Uds. _____ a España.

7. (volver) Estamos seguros de que él _____ mañana.

8. (hacer) Es mejor que yo _____ este trabajo.

9. (conocer) Mamá quiere que nosotros _____ a los invitados.

10. (seguir) Es importante que tú _____ mis consejos.

11. (ver) Queremos que los niños _____ esta película.

12. (estar) Espero que todos Uds. _____ bien.

13. (venir) Me alegro de que Uds. _____ a vernos.

14. (dar) Es necesario que ella se _____ cuenta de esto.

15. (pedir) Él no quiere que nosotros se lo _____ otra vez.

▶ *For more help, see* Subjunctive Mood, *pp. 114–117.*

P   *Complete the following sentences with the imperfect subjunctive of the verbs in parentheses.*

1. (hacer) Quería que Uds. lo _____.

2. (saber) No creíamos que Ud. lo _____.

3. (prestar) Era necesario que tú me lo _____.

4. (ser) Esperaba que la casa _____ más moderna.

5. (pasar) Queríamos que Uds. _____ por nosotros.

6. (ir) Le pedí que _____ conmigo.

7. (recoger) Les mandé que _____ todos los papeles.

8. (decir) Insistieron en que yo se lo _____ todo.

9. (traducir) Me sorprendía que nadie _____ el discurso del presidente.

10. (hablar) Prefería que tú me _____ en español.

11. (dar) Le dije que venías para que te _____ el paquete.

12. (volver) Le avisé antes de que él _____ .

▶ *For more help, see* Imperfect Subjunctive, *pp. 114–118.*

Q   *Complete the following sentences with the pluperfect subjunctive in the **si**-clause and the conditional perfect in the main clause of the verbs given.*

1. Si nosotros lo _____ (saber), _____ (venir).

2. Ella te _____ (ayudar) si tú se lo _____ (pedir).

3. Él no _____ (decírselo) si ella _____ (estar) informada.

4. Yo no _____ (hacerlo) si alguien _____ (decirme) que se prohibía.

5. Si tú _____ (poner) atención, tú _____ (sacar) mejores notas.

6. Si ellos _____ (estudiar), _____ (salir) bien en los exámenes.

7. Si yo _____ (estar) lista, yo _____ (poder) salir con ellos.

8. Tú _____ (comprender) si tú _____ (esforzarse) un poco.

▶ *For more help, see* Pluperfect Subjunctive, *p. 119, and the* Conditional Perfect, *pp. 108–109.*

APPENDIX I

Interrogative Pronouns and Interrogative Adjectives (Comparison)

INTERROGATIVE PRONOUNS
¿qué? ¿cuál? and ¿cuánto(s)/cuánta(s)?

Basically *¿qué?* means *what?*, *¿cuál(es)?* mean(s) *which?* or *which one(s)*, and *¿cuánto(s)?*, *cuánta(s)?* means *how much?* or *how many?*

> *¿**Qué** lees?* → **What** are you reading?
> *¿**Cuál(es)** de estos libros quieres leer?* → **Which** of these books do you want to read?
> *¿**Cuántas** peras quieres? Quiero tres.* → **How many** pears do you want? I want three.

With the verb *ser*, *¿qué?* asks for a definition:

> *¿**Qué** es un gaucho?* → What is a gaucho?
> *¿**Qué** es eso? Es un diccionario.* → What is that? It's a dictionary.

With the verb *ser*, *¿cuál?* asks for information:

> *¿**Cuál** es la fecha?* → What is the date?
> *¿**Cuál** es tu apellido?* → What is your last name?

INTERROGATIVE ADJECTIVES
¿qué?, ¿cuál/es? and ¿cuánto(s)/cuánta(s)?

¿Qué?, ¿cuál/es?, and *¿cuánto(s)/cuánta(s)?* may accompany a noun. In this case they are adjectives, even though they have the same forms as the pronouns:

> *¿**Qué** libros lees?* → What books are you reading?
> *¿**Cuál** libro prefieres?* → Which book do you prefer?
> *¿**Cuántos** periódicos lees todos los días?* → How many newspapers do you read every day?

¿Qué? implies an unlimited choice. *¿Cuáles?* implies a limited one:

> *¿**Qué** libros te gustan?* → What books (any at all) do you like?
> *¿**Cuál** libro prefieres? ¿Éste o ése?* → Which book do you prefer? This one or that one?

With the verb *ser*, *¿cuál?* asks for information about the noun:

> *¿**Cuáles** son los títulos de sus dos libros preferidos?* → What are the titles of your two favorite books?

APPENDIX II
Para and *Por*

The prepositions *para* and *por* have many uses in Spanish. There are several meanings for each. Here we will concentrate on the most common uses, especially the instances in which they may be translated by the English preposition *for*.

1. When *para* means *for:*
   Remember this advice: **Do Use Para Correctly. Follow these Tips:**

   Destination: *Mañana saldré* **para Madrid.** → Tomorrow I will leave **for Madrid.**

   Use: *toallita* **para la cara** → face cloth

   Purpose: *las llantas* **para nieve** → snow tires

   Comparison: *Hablas español bien* **para un norteamericano.** → You speak good Spanish **for an American.**

   Future time (deadline): *Eso es mi trabajo* **para mañana.** → That is my work **for tomorrow.**

   Truth restriction (opinion): **Para mí** *es importante.* → **For me** it's important.

   NOTE: *Para* appears in other expressions in which the English equivalents are not always expressed by *for,* and thus should be treated as idioms or separate vocabulary items. For example:

   estar para → to be about to; to be on the verge of

   para plus an infinitive has other common meanings:

   Leí el libro dos veces **para comprenderlo** *mejor.* → I read the book twice **(in order) to understand it** better.

   Quiero algo **para comer.** → I want something **to eat.**

   para is used with time and dates:

   Llegaré **para las siete.** → I will arrive **by 7 o'clock.**

2. When *por* means *for,* remember:
   Memorizing Funny Rules Becomes Easy Too! *Por* is used when *for* expresses:

   Motive: **por necesidad** → **for** necessity's sake, or **out of** necessity

   Favor (on behalf of): *¿**Por quién** votó Ud.?* → **For whom** did you vote?

   Reason: **por eso** → **for** that reason; **because of** that

   Behalf: *Lo hago* **por María.** → I'm doing it **for María;** on María's behalf

   Exchange: *Me dio un collar* **por mi reloj.** → He gave me a necklace **(in exchange) for** my watch.

   Time length: *Juan va a México* **por tres semanas.** → John is going to Mexico **for three weeks.**

NOTE:

Other common uses of *por:*

1. to express *by* with a verb in the passive voice:

   El libro fue escrito **por Isabel Allende.** → The book was written **by** Isabel Allende.

2. to express *by* in the sense of *by means of* or *with:*

   *televisión **por** cable* → cable television

3. to communicate some fixed expressions:

   ***por** favor* → please

   Por is used in a number of expressions in which we use *per* in English:

   ***por** año* → **per** year   ***por** hora* → per hour   ***por** ciento* → **per** cent

   Por, like *para,* can be used before an infinitive, but the meaning is different:

   *estar **para*** → to be **about** to
   *estar **por*** → to be **inclined** to
   *Estoy **para** comenzar a trabajar.* → I am **about to** start work.
   *No estoy **por** trabajar hoy.* → I **don't feel like** working today.

APPENDIX III
Uses of *Ser* and *Estar*

Ser and *estar* both mean *to be,* but they are used in different situations to convey different impressions.

Ser and *Estar* with Nouns

Ser is used with nouns to tell from where people come, their relationships, and important groups to which they belong. For things, it describes who owns them and of what material they are made. *Estar* is more temporary. It tells where someone or something is at any given time.

	Ser		**Estar**
Origin	*Soy de Chicago.*		
Location of an event	*El concierto **es** en el parque.*	location	*Estoy en la biblioteca.*
		position	*Está a la derecha.*
Groups:			
profession*	*Don Roberto **es** médico.*		
nationality*	*Es español.*		
religion*	*Es católico.*		
politics, etc.*	*Es demócrata.*		
relationship	*Es hermano de Ana.*		
Possession	*Es la casa del señor Gómez.*		
Material	*Este vestido **es** de lana.*		

* With the kind of noun that describes these groups, no determiner is needed, but if you modify the noun, use an indefinite article, *un, una,* as we use *a/an* in English:

*Don Roberto **es un buen** médico.* → Don Roberto **is a good** doctor.

Ser and Estar with Adjectives

Ser describes essential characteristics; how people or things are:

1. fundamentally
2. normally* (what you expect)
3. objectively

Estar describes temporary characteristics; how people or things are:

1. at the moment
2. temporarily
3. in someone's opinion

Examples of the three uses are listed in the table.

1. *Soy morena.* → I am a brunette. (My natural hair color is dark.)	1. *Estoy rubia.* → I am blonde. (At the moment, my hair is blonde.)
2. *Pedro es gordo.* → Peter is fat. (He's always been like that.)	2. *Roberto está gordo.* (At the moment, he is fat; normally he isn't.)
3. *Salvador es guapo.* → Salvador is handsome. (He is a good-looking person.)	3. *Salvador está guapo.* (He is looking particularly handsome today.)
4. *Su casa es vieja.* → Her house is old. (It was built in 1903.)	4. *Su casa no está limpia.* → Her house is not clean. (Normally it is clean. At the moment, it's dirty.)

We might think of these distinctions as the difference between *definition* and *description*. In the following chart, the *ser* column tells us *who* Roberto is. The *estar* column tells *how* he is.

Definition	Description
Es Roberto Robles. → He is Roberto Robles.	
Es de Chicago. → He's from Chicago.	*Está en Londres ahora.* → Now he is in London.
Es americano. → He's an American.	*Está cansado.* → He's tired.
Es moreno. → He's a brunette.	*Está sucio.* → He's dirty.
Es estudiante. → He's a student.	*Está pobre.* → He's broke.
Es católico. → He's Catholic.	
Es un amigo de Ud. → He's a friend of yours.	

Ser and Estar with Verbs

Ser plus Past Participle
(to describe an action)
Fue matado por un ladrón. → He was killed by a thief.

Estar plus Past Participle
(to describe the present state)
La ventana está cerrada. → The window is closed.

Estar plus Present Participle
(to form the present progressive)
Enrique está preguntándose. → Henry is wondering.

OTHER VERBS IN EXPRESSIONS IN WHICH TO BE IS USED IN ENGLISH

tener   *Tengo hambre.* → **I am** hungry.
         Tiene 18 años. → He **is** eighteen years old.

hacer   *Hace muchos años que . . .* → It has **been** many years since . . .
         Hace sol. → It **is** sunny out.

haber   *Hay un jardín detrás de mi casa.* → There **is** a garden behind my house.

* What is "normal" may change. As in the example above, Pedro has always been fat; this is normal for him. If he loses weight, we will say at first, *"Está delgado."* With time, though, we will get used to a thin Pedro. Gradually we will start to say *"Es delgado."* His new shape will have become what we expect to see.

Answer Key

Nouns and Determiners

A 1. la 2. el 3. el 4. el 5. las 6. los 7. los 8. la 9. el 10. la

B 1. una 2. una 3. unas 4. un 5. un 6. unas 7. una 8. un 9. una 10. unos

C 1. unos 2. los 3. La 4. Unos 5. un 6. El 7. Los 8. unas 9. Las 10. unos

Pronouns

A 1. nosotros, nosotras 2. yo 3. él, ella, Ud. 4. vosotros, vosotras 5. ellos, ellas, Uds.
6. él, ella, Ud. 7. yo 8. tú 9. vosotros, vosotras 10. ellos, ellas, Uds. 11. tú
12. nosotros, nosotras

B 1. Los tenemos. 2. La preparan. 3. Las reparo. 4. ¿No lo bebes? 5. No la conocen.
6. Ya las leí. 7. Los llevamos al zoológico. 8. ¿Los compraron Uds.? 9. Lo vendieron.
10. El niño lo rompió.

C 1. Hazlo. 2. No los sirvas. 3. La quiero comer., Quiero comerla.
4. ¿La debo cerrar?, ¿Debo cerrarla? 5. Pónganlos en la mesa. 6. Ábralas.
7. ¿Las podemos ver?, ¿Podemos verlas? 8. Los estudiantes lo piensan estudiar.,
Los estudiantes piensan estudiarlo. 9. ¿Lo puede Ud. traducir?, ¿Puede Ud. traducirlo?
10. Sácala.

D 1. lo 2. me 3. nos 4. me 5. te

E 1. Se los envían. 2. Se lo lee. 3. Dáselos. 4. Se lo mando. 5. ¿Puedes
devolvérmelos? (¿Me los puedes devolver?) 6. Se lo enseña. 7. Te las voy a mostrar.
(Voy a mostrártelas.) 8. A Ud. se lo voy a vender. (A Ud. voy a vendérselo.)
9. Me lo pongo. 10. Dígamela. 11. Voy a preparártelo. (Te lo voy a preparar.)
12. ¿Se la explicas?

F 1. nosotros 2. ti 3. mí 4. Ud. 5. Uds. 6. mí

G 1. la suya 2. la nuestra 3. los míos 4. las tuyas 5. el suyo 6. el suyo 7. las suyas
8. el suyo 9. la mía 10. los suyos 11. el tuyo (el suyo) 12. la mía

H 1. a 2. b 3. c 4. d 5. a 6. d 7. e 8. b

I 1. Este libro y ése. 2. Estas casas y aquéllas. 3. Estos restaurantes son buenos,
pero aquéllos son mejores. 4. Ese teléfono celular es bueno, pero éste es excelente.
5. Me gustan los coches, pero no me gusta aquél. 6. Estos jardines y ésos tienen flores
hermosas. 7. ¿Quieres aquellos pasteles o éstos? 8. Esa bicicleta es más cara que ésta.

J 1. A quién 2. Qué 3. A quiénes 4. Cuál 5. De qué 6. Con quién 7. En qué
8. Cuántos 9. Quién 10. Qué 11. A quién 12. Cuánto 13. Para quiénes
14. Cuáles

Adjectives

A 1. interesante, interesante, interesantes   2. blanca, blancos, blancas   3. español, española, españolas   4. andaluza, andaluces, andaluzas   5. buen, buena, buenas   6. joven, jóvenes, jóvenes   7. fácil, fáciles, fáciles   8. algún, alguna, algunas   9. alemán, alemana, alemanes   10. gran, gran, grandes

B 1. tercer   2. ninguna   3. mal   4. primera   5. algún   6. gran   7. tercera   8. ningún   9. primer   10. buen

C 1. San   2. Santa   3. Santo   4. Santa   5. San   6. Santa   7. Santo   8. San   9. Santa   10. San

D 1. un pobre hombre   2. una vieja amiga   3. un antiguo general   4. una ciudad antigua   5. una gran mujer   6. un hombre pobre   7. una muchacha grande   8. un vecino viejo

E 1. Jaime es más inteligente que Raúl.   2. Mi hermana es menos aplicada que mi hermano.   3. Es el mejor libro de la biblioteca.   4. El metro es más rápido que el autobús.   5. (Él) es el peor estudiante de la escuela (del colegio).   6. Mi curso es menos interesante que el curso de ellos (que su curso, que el curso suyo).

F 1. aquellas mujeres   2. este libro   3. esa mesa   4. esos aviones   5. aquel coche (carro)   6. estas sillas   7. esas ventanas   8. aquella puerta   9. esta página   10. aquellos autobuses   11. esos trenes   12. estos exámenes

G 1. su libro   2. mi escuela (colegio)   3. su casa   4. nuestra traducción   5. sus jardines   6. tus ideas   7. sus cuadernos   8. mis tareas (deberes)   9. tu composición   10. su historia

Adverbs

A 1. fácilmente   2. nerviosamente   3. maravillosamente   4. bien   5. lentamente   6. claramente   7. naturalmente   8. cuidadosamente   9. responsablemente   10. ferozmente

B 1. Él no trabaja.   2. Él no trabaja más.   3. Él no trabaja nunca (jamás). (Él nunca (jamás) trabaja.)   4. Nadie trabaja. (No trabaja nadie.)   5. Ella no aprende nada.   6. No vemos ni a Paula ni a Carmen.

Prepositions

A 1. a   2. cerca de   3. en   4. delante de   5. debajo de   6. antes de

B 1. de   2. a   3. a   4. X   5. a   6. por   7. a   8. de   9. a   10. X   11. de   12. a

Verbs

A 1. diciendo, dicho   2. yendo, ido   3. viendo, visto   4. muriendo, muerto   5. abriendo, abierto   6. poniendo, puesto   7. sintiendo, sentido   8. durmiendo, dormido   9. escribiendo, escrito   10. rompiendo, roto   11. haciendo, hecho   12. volviendo, vuelto

B 1. caminan   2. aprendo   3. Entiendes   4. piensan   5. siento   6. muestras   7. juegan   8. pide   9. repite   10. permitimos   11. comemos   12. sigo   13. hago   14. traigo   15. estoy

C 1. está trabajando   2. estoy volviendo   3. estás escribiendo   4. está caminando
5. estamos pidiendo   6. están durmiendo   7. estoy oyendo   8. estás mintiendo

D 1. Hablaba con su novia.   2. Terminábamos nuestro trabajo.   3. Ella hacía un café.
4. Esperaba a mis amigos.   5. El niño dormía.   6. Estábamos preocupados.
7. Vendías tu casa.   8. Ella trabajaba en esta oficina.   9. Estudiábamos nuestras
lecciones.   10. Seguían por esta calle.   11. Iban al centro.   12. Veía películas
en la tele.   13. Escribías una carta.   14. Ud. leía mucho.   15. Salía.   16. Ella estaba
en el centro.   17. Era inteligente.   18. Nunca perdías nada.

E 1. estaban comiendo   2. estabas viendo   3. estábamos siendo   4. yo estaba hablando
5. estábamos saliendo   6. estaban regresando   7. ella estaba llegando   8. estabas
viviendo

F 1. compramos   2. Prendiste   3. busqué   4. tuve   5. se sintió   6. durmió
7. Escribiste   8. empecé   9. puso   10. hizo   11. dijeron   12. tradujo   13. vinieron
14. fue   15. supiste   16. quise   17. di   18. pagué   19. comimos   20. dieron
21. estuvo   22. caminaron   23. Fuiste   24. pudimos

G 1. No sé si saldrán.   2. No sé si podrá(s).   3. No sé si perderá.   4. No sé si lo haré.
5. No sé si lo sabremos.   6. No sé si lo diré.   7. No sé si abriré la puerta.
8. No sé si pondremos la mesa.   9. No sé si habrá una reunión.   10. No sé si querrá(s).

H 1. tendrían   2. pondría   3. echaríamos   4. harían   5. escribirían   6. saldrías
7. cabría   8. diría   9. venderíamos   10. querrías   11. habría   12. daría

I 1. Ya he abierto las ventanas.   2. Ya han puesto la mesa.   3. Ya hemos hecho ejercicio.
4. Ya ha llamado.   5. Ya he pedido una pizza.   6. Ya han (hemos) visto la película.
7. Ya han vuelto.   8. Ya hemos escrito el mensaje.

J 1. Ya había salido.   2. Ya había hecho el té.   3. Ya habían jugado.   4. Ya habían vuelto.
5. Ya habíamos hablado.   6. Ya había telefoneado.   7. Ya lo habían visto.
8. Ya habíamos comido.

K 1. ¿Cómo lo habrán sabido?   2. ¿Cómo habré ganado?   3. ¿Cómo habrán llegado?
4. ¿Cómo habremos sacado el premio?   5. ¿Cómo habrás conseguido el trabajo?
6. ¿Cómo habrá reparado el juguete?

L 1. La pelota es tirada por los niños.   2. El mensaje fue escrito por Pablo.
3. El informe ha sido estudiado por los expertos.   4. Esta cantante es admirada
por (de) todos.   5. Los criminales fueron arrestados por la policía.   6. La cena ha
sido hecha por mi abuela.   7. Un nuevo estadio será construido por la ciudad.
8. Un comité será organizado por el director.

M 2. Dámelo., No me lo des.   3. Escríbele., No le escribas.   4. Sal., No salgas.
5. Dínoslo., No nos lo digas.   6. Hazlo., No lo hagas.   7. Véndesela., No se la vendas.
8. Ponlo., No lo pongas.

N 2. Dígamelo., No me lo diga.   3. Ábralas., No las abra.   4. Óigala., No la oiga.
5. Véalos., No los vea.   6. Hágalo., No lo haga.   7. Apréndalos., No los aprenda.
8. Conózcalo., No lo conozca.

O 1. pueda   2. entienda   3. quieren   4. sepas   5. escoja   6. vayan   7. vuelve   8. haga
9. conozcamos   10. sigas   11. vean   12. estén   13. vengan   14. dé   15. pidamos

P 1. hicieran   2. supiera   3. prestaras   4. fuera   5. pasaran   6. fuera   7. recogieran
8. dijera   9. tradujera   10. hablaras   11. diera   12. volviera

Q 1. hubiéramos sabido, habríamos venido   2. habría ayudado, hubieras pedido
3. no se lo habría dicho, hubiera estado   4. no lo habría hecho, me hubiera dicho
5. hubieras puesto, habrías sacado   6. hubieran estudiado, habrían salido
7. hubiera estado, habría podido   8. habrías comprendido, te hubieras esforzado